Institutional Commitment to Global Engagement

Cross-Cultural Reflections of Faculty, Students, Staff, and Alumnae at Spelman College

Edited by

'Dimeji R. Togunde and Krishna Bista

First Published 2023

by

STAR Scholars

In collaboration with

Open Journals in Education

Journal of International Students

Category

Education/Higher Education

Series

Comparative and International Education

Editors

'Dimeji R. Togunde | Krishna Bista

ISBN: 978-1-957480-13-8

Library of Congress Control Number: 2021943751

Library of Congress US Programs, Law, and Literature Division Cataloging in Publication Program 101 Independence Avenue, S.E. Washington, DC 20540-4283

Printed in the United States of America

Facts and opinions published in this book express solely the opinions of the respective authors. Authors are responsible for their citing of sources and the accuracy of their references and bibliographies. The editor, series editor or the publisher cannot be held responsible for any lack or possible violations of third parties' rights.

Copyright © 2023 by STAR Scholars

All rights reserved.

No portion of this book may be reproduced in any form without written permission from the publisher or authors/editors except as permitted by U.S. copyright law.

STAR Scholars Titles

We seek to explore new ideas and best practices related to international and comparative education from the US and around the world, and from a wide range of academic fields, including leadership studies, technology, general education, and area and cultural studies. STAR Scholars publishes some titles in collaboration with Routledge, Palgrave MacMillan, Open Journals in Education, *Journal of International Students*, and other university presses. At STAR Scholars Network, we aim to amplify the voices of underrepresented scholars, epistemologies, and perspectives. We are committed to an inclusion of a diversity of racial, ethnic, and cultural backgrounds and are particularly interested in proposals from scholars who identify with countries in the Global South. More information at https://starscholars.org/open-access/

Recently Published Books

1. *Chinese Students and the Experience of International Doctoral Study in STEM*
2. *Developing Intercultural Competence in Higher Education*
3. *International Student Mobility to and from the Middle East*
4. *Inequalities in Study Abroad and Student Mobility*
5. *The Experiences of International Faculty in Institutions of Higher Education*
6. *International Students at US Community Colleges*
7. *Critical Perspectives on Equity and Social Mobility in Study Abroad*
8. *Online Teaching, Learning and Virtual Experiences in Global Higher Education*
9. *International Student Support and Engagement in Higher Education*

About the Book

This book is a testimony of Spelman College's commitment to global citizenship, documenting cross-cultural and international experiences and reflections of domestic students who studied abroad, international students' experiences, Alumnae who studied abroad or have lived abroad and faculty and staff who have lived abroad or led students abroad. This book distinctively reveals life stories of global engagements that no one else could tell but the contributors who bring life experiences through their international visits. Through a well-curated and engaging collection of narrative stories, this book captures the richness that comes from crossing boundaries, understanding cultural differences, and embracing the knowledge that comes from encounters with disparate perspectives. It also highlights first-hand reflections of the Spelman constituencies who have embraced the institutional vision to explore the wider world, modeling the importance of thinking globally and understanding the world through more international connections.

The book shows the diversity of essayists, the diversity of reflections, and the diversity of reflections. The emerging themes include a deep appreciation of the opportunity to study in the United States, new ways of cultivating friendships, dealing with culture shock, joy of developing a sense of belonging, opportunity to enjoy freedom in America, creating a "new family" away from home, self-discovery, fighting racism and learning more about it, building resilience, and cultivating success and cross-cultural understanding. This book provides direct evidence regarding how individuals encounter new socio-political, economic, and cultural milieus that shape their beliefs, world views, identities and social construction of gender roles. We hope that the book serves as a reservoir of knowledge by adding to these original cross-cultural perspectives from a prominent Historically Black College.

Editors

'Dimeji R. Togunde, Ph.D. Vice Provost for Global Education & Professor of International Studies, Spelman College, Atlanta, Georgia, USA

Krishna Bista, Ed.D. Professor of Higher Education, Morgan State University, Maryland, USA

Overview of Global Engagement at Spelman

Spelman College is a highly selective, historically black college that empowers women to change the world. Located in Atlanta, Georgia, USA, it was established in 1881 and currently enrolls approximately 2100 women undergraduates. A global leader in the education of women of African descent, Spelman offers a holistic education founded on academic excellence in the liberal arts and sciences and the intellectual, creative, ethical, and leadership development of its students.

Spelman has a long-standing commitment to expose students to the world around them through teaching, research, and service-learning as this is core to our mission to develop leaders who can effectively engage the many cultures of the world. At its founding, one of Spelman's earliest students, Nora Gordon studied in the Congo in 1888, while Flora Zeto came from the Congo as an international student to study at Spelman in 1915. The legacy of these two women shapes the Spelman mission to expand its reach of internationalization beyond international student exchange to encompass a wide array of initiatives summarized in this introductory chapter.

The institutional commitment to expand students' cross-cultural understanding gained momentum in 1981 when the office of study abroad was officially established and headed by Dr. Margery Ganz as director. The combination of her leadership, partnerships with the Office of Institutional Advancement and study abroad providers, donations, scholarship endowments provided by several alumnae, trustees, and friends of the College have led to substantial increase in study abroad participation from 3 in 1982 to 159 in 2011.

The 2011-2012 academic year was a turning point in the history and growth of global engagement at Spelman due to the importance of three major institutional commitment factors:

Implementation and the Institutionalization of the Quality Enhancement Plan (QEP: 2011-2016):

To demonstrate Spelman's commitment to internationalization, the College decided to leverage accreditation through the Quality Enhancement Plan (QEP), an initiative mandated by our accreditation body, the Southern Association of Colleges and Schools Commission on Colleges (SACSCOC) to enhance international initiatives. This agency requires all institutions in the Southern Region of the United States to develop a Quality Enhancement Plan (QEP) that addresses a well-defined topic related to enhancing student learning as part of the re-accreditation process and to submit an impact report at the end of the fifth year. After several meetings of all stakeholders and a careful evaluation of three contending topical areas, it was approved that Spelman's first QEP should be titled *Spelman Going Global: Developing Intercultural Competence*, championed by the 9th President, Dr. Beverly Daniel Tatum. It aimed to provide students with the skills they will need to navigate diverse global cultural landscapes and to be successful as global leaders. Its goal was to foster student interest in civic engagement and social responsibility for local and global communities.

To determine the transformative impact of study abroad experience and assess students' intercultural competence, Spelman has developed two learning outcomes across study abroad programs:

• Identify differences and commonalities of two world societies based on political, economic, social and/or cultural values during each study-travel experience (Knowledge Component).

• Develop a personal definition of cultural engagement that reflects openness to cultural difference (Attitude Component)

These two learning outcomes were developed with the theoretical guidance provided by the Deardorff Process Model of Intercultural Competence (Deardorff, 2006). For more information about the Intercultural Competence Model and how Spelman has assessed the two learning outcomes and the results, see Togunde and Fall, 2017.

A mission-driven and an outcome-based initiative, *Spelman Going Global!* was designed and supported by two consecutive strategic plans (2010-2017 and 2017-2023) to enhance student learning through global study-travel experiences connected to the College's liberal arts curriculum, the Spelman MILE (My Integrated Learning Experience). Led by the former provost, Dr. Johnnella E. Butler, the Spelman MILE "integrates and connects curricular and co-curricular experiences to provide students with the intellectual foundation, knowledge, skills, and competencies for continued intellectual growth, leadership, success, and service".

While the overarching goal of the *Going Global* was to ensure that every Spelman student had a global travel experience prior to graduation, it was embedded with specific study abroad participation target goal for each year. The Going Global initiative was able to increase study abroad from 218 in 2011-2012 to 402 in 2015-2016, a jump of 84% during the five-year period. Furthermore, study abroad destinations also increased from 22 in 2012 to 35 in 2016, an increase of 59%. Moreover, the diversity of student participation across the academic divisions indicated that except for the Fine Arts Division, student global travels expanded significantly beyond the minimum 50% increase (Unpublished QEP report Submitted by Spelman College to SACSCOC, 2016). Thus, serving as a catalyst, Spelman has leveraged the institutionalization of the QEP to advance its mission and build on its historical legacy to develop a more elaborate global education agenda that enjoys the support of several campus stakeholders- faculty, students, staff, alumnae, and board of trustees.

After a successful review of the QEP Report by SACSCOC and the institutionalization of the Going Global!, the following years witnessed an accelerated increase in study abroad participation from 218 in 2012 to 474 in 2019, an increase of 117%. Indeed, 77% of the graduating class of 2019 had at least a study abroad experience. Having clearly elevated its brand as a leader in campus internationalization, Spelman now sends more black students to study abroad than any other baccalaureate institution in the United States (IIE 2019).

A Philanthropic Investment of $17 million Endowment:

Dr. Beverly Daniel Tatum's vision for launching the *Going Global*! initiative was strongly supported by the generous gift of $17 million endowment from Spelman College Trustee, Ms. Ronda Stryker and her husband, Mr. William Johnston. It remains one of the largest gifts ever donated to support global engagement in the field of international education. With half of the student body drawn from Pell eligible households, this is a momentous commitment. As a result, the College has been able to make the culture of global engagement so integral to the teaching and learning environment.

Furthermore, the 10th President of Spelman College, Dr. Mary Schmidt Campbell, provided significant financial support to expand Spelman's internationalization efforts. During her tenure, enhancing global learning was at the core of the strategic plan. One of its pillars, *Deliver the Spelman Promise*, aimed to ensure that every Spelmanite graduates with a competitive edge, anchored in a robust education that prepares students for life and career through curricular and co-curricular activities. According to Dr. Campbell, "students are encouraged to understand the study of their majors against the backdrop of a broad globalism, and when they arrive at Spelman, they are promised that study abroad will be accessible to them, irrespective of their socio-economic background" (Campbell, 2017). While the College has been able to accomplish a great deal from the proceeds from the endowment, its laudable goals have pushed the institution to seek additional grants from the Mellon Foundation (Award #41100113), Department of Education, Institutional Services (Title III HBCU B, SAFRA), National Science Foundation (Award #0963629), Carnegie and Rockefeller Foundation grants and other sources, such as the Associated Colleges of the South.

Moreover, Spelman's 11th President, Dr. Helene D. Gayle, who assumed her role in July, 2022, has been profoundly passionate about global education and the imperative that organizations play tangible roles in finding solutions to pressing global challenges in areas of health, poverty, and gender inequality. President Gayle is poised to expand Spelman footprints in global engagement by enhancing the opportunities for domestic students to study abroad, boosting faculty global research, promoting curriculum internationalization, and supporting campus intellectual dialogues on topics that have global significance. She is "thinking big on how Spelman can be seen as a true global resource, where more women from the African Diaspora can come to Spelman to access the opportunities for Spelman education through strategic partnerships, international student exchange, and intentional marketing of our strengths as an institution reputed for its academic excellence" (Gayle, 2022). She aims to deepen global connections in several aspects of our signature programs, such as the Center for Black Entrepreneurship, Social Justice Program, Innovation Lab, eSpelman, and Center of Excellence for Minority Women in STEM. With that compelling vision and global mindset, the institutional commitment to global education bodes well for even a higher level of success.

The Establishment of the Gordon-Zeto Center for Global Education:

The implementation of the Spelman Going Global! initiative began in 2011 with the establishment of the Gordon-Zeto Center for Global Education as an infrastructure that provides coherence and centralization of all international initiatives on the Campus. Named after Nora Gordon and Flora Zeto, the Center embodies the College's commitment of promoting students' engagement with world cultures. Established with a philanthropic investment of $17 million endowment, the Center is led by its founding dean, who currently serves as vice provost for global education to provide vision, strategic leadership for Spelman's international initiatives and the assessment of students' global learning outcomes.

The Center manages a variety of global engagement that includes semester abroad, faculty-mentored international research (through the G-STEM Program), short-term summer faculty-led study abroad programs, international internship, students' participation in Model United Nations (through the International Affairs Center), and service learning abroad, in partnership with the Bonner Center for Civic Engagement. The Gordon-Zeto Center also works with the Office of Student Affairs, who regularly organizes Student Affairs Global Engagement (SAGE) to a variety of international destinations.

Through its wide array of initiatives, the Gordon-Zeto Center has been able to promote the culture of global learning, reduce the cost barrier, ease family fears, and create champions (Togunde and Fall, 2019). The center also manages the International Student Services & Programming. And while the number of international students' needs to be strengthened, they bring their cultural values and diversity of ideas to the classroom, broaden cross-cultural communication, and serve as vessels for promoting intercultural competence.

The Gordon-Zeto Center also leads the efforts in building strategic international partnerships to support student and faculty global engagements, hosting international scholars and lectures on global topics, promoting faculty development initiatives that include the internationalization of the curriculum and providing funds to support international research. The breadth and depth of Spelman faculty global engagement are also manifested in other interrelated ways that include international conferences, seminars, and pedagogical workshops, spending sabbaticals abroad, internationally focused publications and a significant presence of foreign-born faculty, who bring diverse perspectives and enrich cross-cultural understanding in and out of the Campus. For more on the impact of campus internationalization on faculty at Spelman, (see Togunde and Fall, 2023).

To conclude, in recognition of its success as a hub for global learning, Spelman has won several awards from professional organizations in international education, including Senator Paul Simon award for campus internationalization in 2017, Excellence in Diversity and Inclusion in International Education (EDIIE Award) from Diversity Abroad Network in 2018, and the Seal of Excellence in Generation Study Abroad from IIE in 2019. Furthermore, Spelman has been recognized consecutively for five years by the Institute of International Education (IIE) Open Doors Report among the top baccalaureate institutions sending students abroad (ranked #15 in 2020).

Between 2019 and fall 2022, the pandemic temporarily halted our momentum in global travels. But, we pivoted and developed innovative approaches to global learning, such as virtual global internship for students; virtual exchange, which enables faculty to create an opportunity for students to engage with students and speakers in another country on a topic/theme or module embedded in a globally focused course; and "Connecting Globally while Grounded at Home" (Global At Home) research projects for faculty (For more information on how these viable and accessible virtual strategic initiatives can advance internationalization, (see Togunde and Harvey, 2022). Nonetheless, Spelman has remained committed to its proven goals of increasing students' ability to communicate across cultures; challenging their biases and assumptions while they learn more about racism against blacks in other countries; helping in the development of their identity through heritage connection and interaction with other black peoples in the African diaspora; and positively shaping their academic and career trajectory (See Togunde and Fall, 2017).

'Dimeji R. Togunde, Ph.D.

Vice-Provost for Global Education & Professor of International Studies at Spelman College, Atlanta, Georgia USA.

His Recent Publications on Spelman Global Engagement

2023 **Togunde**, D. and Fall, R. "Understanding the Growth, Assessment Methods and Transformative Impact of Study Abroad at Spelman College." Forthcoming in Stevenson,

A. and Abraham, K. (eds), The Half Yet to Be Told: Study Abroad and HBCUs. The Forum on Education Abroad Standards in Action Book Series.

2023 **Togunde**, D. and Fall, R. "Faculty Internationalization: The Impact of Faculty-Led Study Abroad Programs on Faculty at Spelman College"". Forthcoming in Stevenson, A. and Abraham, K. (eds), The Half Yet to Be Told: Study Abroad and HBCUs. The Forum on Education Abroad Standards in Action Book Series.

2022 Charles, H. and **Togunde**, D. "What Counts as Internationalization and For Whom: Comprehensive Internationalization at Historically Black Colleges and Universities. In Bista, K. and Pinder, A, (eds). Reimagining Internationalization and International Initiatives at Historically Black Colleges and Universities (pp.45-60). Palgrave MacMillan

2022 **Togunde**, D. and Charles, H. "Universalizing Internationalization at Historically Black Colleges and Universities Through Virtual Learning". In Bista, K. and Pinder, A, (eds). Reimagining Internationalization and International Initiatives at Historically Black Colleges and Universities (pp.63-72). Palgrave MacMillan

2021 **Togunde**, D; Lewis, A. and Fall, R. "Practical Ways to Decolonizing Education Studies Majors and Global Learning at Spelman College". In Colon, C., Gristwood, A. and Woolf, M. (Eds.), In Empires of the Mind? (Post)colonialism and Decolonizing Education Abroad (pp. 119-127). Chicago, IL: CAPA: The Global Education Network Occasional Publication No 9.

2020 Charles, H. and **Togunde**, D. "HBCUs, Internationalization and Re-envisioning the Post- Pandemic Institutional Landscape" In International Educator (NAFSA: Association of International Educators, December 2020 Edition. https://www.nafsa.org/ie-magazine/2020/12/8/historically-black-colleges-and-universities-2020-perspective

2019 **Togunde**, D., Crosby Brown, D., Phillips Lewis, K. & Fall, R. "A Curricular model for facilitating intercultural competence development for student learning abroad at Spelman College." Published by Diversity Abroad Network September 12, 2019. https://www.diversitynetwork.org/page/Articles

2019 **Togunde**, D., & Fall, R. "Success in Campus Internationalization at Spelman College: Lessons for Other Institutions". In Colon, C., Gristwood, A. and Woolf, M. (Eds.), Borders, Mobility, and Migration, (pp. 169-181). Chicago, IL: CAPA: The Global Education Network Occasional Publication No 8.

2017 McCormack K, **Togunde** D, Galvao T, Clay, K and Burnett M. "Enhancing Global Research and Education (G-STEM) at Spelman College Chapter 4 in STEM and Social Justice: Teaching and Learning in Diverse Settings – A Global Perspective. Cheryl B. Leggon and Michael S. Gaines (eds); SPRINGER.

2017 **Togunde**, D. and Fall R. "Spelman Going Global: Developing Intercultural Competence through International Travel Experience. Case Study #25 (pp. 269-274) in Intercultural Competence in International Higher Education. Darla K. Deardorff and Lily A. Arasaratnam (eds); ROUTLEDGE.

2015 **Togunde**, D. "The Spelman Model for Enhancing Global Research in STEM Disciplines (with Kai McCormack, Cassia Galvao and Karen Clay) in IMPACT of the Arcadia Experience Abroad: http://arcadiaabroad.uberflip.com/i/508572-impact-magazine-2015/5

Acknowledgments

This book grew out of the necessity to contribute to the growing scholarship on the transformative impact of global engagement. Without the painstaking efforts of thirty-two contributors who provided cross-cultural reflections, the completion of this book will not have been possible. I also thank the commitment of several Spelman College presidents – Drs. Beverly Daniel Tatum, Mary Schmidt Campbell, and Helene D. Gayle to the Spelman mission and for the opportunity to work with them. Their recognition of the importance of a globalized campus have spurred fund-raising efforts, consecutive strategic plans, and visions for innovative international initiatives. While I didn't have the opportunity to work with Drs. Donald M. Stewart and Johnnetta B. Cole, their leadership in revitalizing the academic curriculums through the establishment of the Study Abroad Office and Africa Diaspora & the World Program respectively, laid the solid foundations upon which we have built the Spelman Global Engagement. The support of the Spelman Board of Trustees is immeasurably appreciated for recognizing the importance of global education as imperative for student success and leadership in the 21st Century.

My gratitude extends to several faculty who teach global education courses, lead students abroad, encourage students to study abroad, conduct research abroad or examine the interconnectedness of local and global issues. Without our fruitful collaboration, Spelman will not be able to boast of its impressive accomplishments that have received national attention. It certainly "takes a village to a raise a child", so my heartfelt appreciation goes to dedicated colleagues on my team, past and present: Drs. Dorian B. Cosby, who served as the inaugural director of cultural orientation, Margery Ganz, professor emerita and former director of study abroad, Kathleen Phillips Lewis, former director of cultural orientation, Alix Pierre, former director of cultural orientation, Sara Busdiecker, chair of the international studies program and director of international affairs center, Kai McCormack, director of G-STEM Program, Karen E. Clay, director of semester study abroad and cultural orientation, and Letoyia S tarr-Irving, international student services and faculty-led programs manager. I am indebted to both Mrs. Rokhaya Fall, former Coordinator of international student services and faculty-led programs, and Ms. Renee

ACKNOWLEDGMENTS

Jones, former coordinator of semester study abroad, for their diligence and dedication to the goals of the Gordon-Zeto Center. Special thanks to Dr. Tinaz Pavri, professor of political science, division chair for the social sciences, and founding director of the Asian Studies Program, for her knack for collaboration in advancing student international exchange and Asian Studies curricular and co-curricular activities.

Thanks to Ms. Chandra McCrary, for helping us with technology to support our initiatives. I am also grateful to Ms. Dawn Alston and her team in the Office of Business Affairs for supporting our numerous demands for creating new study-travel accounts. Ms. Pat Johnson has been so helpful in meeting our deadlines by cutting checks for faculty and students within a short notice. The encouragements from Drs. Aditi Pai, interim vice provost for faculty affairs, Karen Brakke, professor psychology and co-director of Teaching Resource & Research Center, Tasha Inniss, associate provost for research, Terri Reed, chief of staff, Office of Public Relations & Communications, Gloria Wade Gayles, eminent professor & founding director of Spelman Independent Scholars (SIS), Virginia "Ginger" Floyd, associate clinical professor at the Morehouse School of Medicine, John Brown, the Registrar, Soraya Mekerta, associate professor of French, Deans of Undergraduate Studies- Drs. Desiree Pedescleaux, DeKimberlen Neely, Geneva Baxter, and Stacy Washington, Manager of Special Programs are beyond expression.

I have benefitted greatly from the insights and support of my former and current supervisors. I so much appreciated the steadfast support and guidance of Dr. Johnnella E. Butler, former provost, and professor emerita. Her clear understanding of the value of liberal arts education was instrumental to the design of the Spelman MILE, which anchors Spelman's global engagement. I also thank Dr. Myra Burnett, former interim provost for her guidance when I was directing the College's first Quality Enhancement Plan - *Spelman Going Global!* Prof. Sharon L. Davies, former provost, was a great supporter of our work and her ability to connect the dots was highly cherished. Moreover, Dr. Dolores Bradley Brennan, current interim provost, has been unwavering in her support of our global education agenda. Yet, I will always be grateful to Ms. Helga H. Greenfield, former chief of staff and associate vice-president for Title III and government relations, for bringing the federal funds that have supported global education and other strategic initiatives, embodied in the College's strategic plans. A consummate professional, her meritorious service to Spelman College deserves recognition.

I really appreciate my co-editor, Prof. Krishna Bista, for his brilliance, energy, dynamism, and enthusiasm to work with me on this project. And finally, to my wife, Agnes, for her love, prayers, and support of my career; and to our three adult daughters: Temitope, Abisola, and Olapeju, for being my cheerleaders.

'Dimeji R. Togunde, Ph.D.

Essay Reviewers

Special thanks to the following reviewers who assisted us in reviewing manuscripts received for this book. It could not be possible to finalize the selected chapters without their evaluations and constructive feedback.

Reviewers

Prashanti Chennamsetti . Marguerite Falcon . Roshan Paudel . Karen Irving . Patricia Timmons . Wauseca Briscoe . Fatima Babih . Tolulope Ajayi . Kenneth Robell . Dedra Adams-Johnson . Sanoya Amienyi . Kristin Mosura . Michael Ashleman . Julie Cappo . Lori . Jason Couch . Elizabeth Sanborn . Stephanie Cheramie . Eleni (Helen) Coyle . Kristin Mosura . Crystal Mallett . Kristina Zachary . Madison . Raborn Rachelle LeBlanc . Haley Collins . Karen Large . Stephania Lenard . Nathaly Caraballo . Lisa Rhoden . Connar Franklin . Jasmine Pittman . Christy M. Green . Avis Sampson . Lindsey Clark . Nicole Schoenborn . Danielle Singleton

Praise for This Book

This book provides valuable lessons learned from Spelman College experience with global engagement. Hopefully, it will be useful to other institutions that are on a similar journey to assure that their students are prepared to be global citizens. In their own words, cross-cultural reflections offer deep, rich, and compelling perspectives to enhance our understanding of the transformative power of global travels.

Dr. Helene D. Gayle, President, Spelman College

Thanks to the leadership of Dr. 'Dimeji Togunde, Spelman College has developed a nationally recognized global engagement program that has become a signature aspect of the College's academic offerings. Working closely with faculty and institutional partners in the United States and abroad, Spelman's internationalization initiatives, under Dr. Togunde's leadership, has deepened and expanded the college's already strong majors in all of its four divisions. With this new book, *Institutional Commitment to Global Engagement: Cross Cultural Reflections of Faculty, Staff, Students and Alumnae at Spelman College*, Togunde and Bista have assembled an important set of reflections that provide critical insights into how to design, implement and support a study abroad program that is equitably available to all students.

Dr. Mary Schmidt Campbell, President Emerita, Spelman College

Spelman College made an institutional commitment to global learning and has delivered on it in a myriad of ways. This rich tapestry of narratives inspired by global experiences affirms the educational importance of creating meaningful international travel opportunities for every student and sets a stellar example for other institutions to follow.

Dr. Beverly Daniel Tatum, President Emerita, Spelman College

This book illustrates a profoundly encouraging success story at Spelman College. Through first-person narratives, it offers an insight into the various ways in which international experience has enriched the consciousness of their colleagues. The reader reconnects with the core purposes of education abroad: an interaction between the politics of identity and journeys into unfamiliar spaces, those within and those beyond the individual.

Dr. Michael Woolf, Deputy President for Strategic Development, CAPA : The Global Education Network

Institutional Commitment to Global Engagement highlights a variety of voices and experiences from, now, experts within various disciplines, all with a shared commitment to global education at HBCUs. The book confirms how strategic planning and visionary action can lead to transformative insight and opportunities for students, faculty and administrators within HBCUs, as well as other institutions.

Andre P. Stevenson, Professor of Social Work and Director of the Office of International Programs, Elizabeth City State University

With this compelling collection of personal narratives and reflections, Togunde and Bista chart the life-alerting impact of intercultural exchange in the development of globally-minded citizens. The testimony of the transformative experiences recounted in this volume speak to Spelman College's vision for global engagement and offer a template for others to follow.

Richard Johnson, Professor of English and Humanities, Harper College

This book offers a convincing narrative of the transformative power of global engagement. More importantly however, it demonstrates how much more can be achieved when institutions elect to become strategically engaged in helping to facilitate such experiences. Accessible, engaging, and spoken from the lived experiences of the authors, this volume offers a vision that should inspire institutions, particularly HBCUs, to engage in what may arguably be the most urgent imperative for the 21st century.

Harvey Charles, Professor of International Education, University at Albany, SUNY

This informative and inspiring collection of essays curated by Togunde and Bista not only showcases the Spelman Community's deep commitment to global engagement, but it also provides practical examples on how institutions can creatively weave the disciplines of intercultural learning, race relations and personal agency together as a way of enhancing global education and ultimately improving the human exp*erience.*

Jennifer Clinton, CEO, Cultural Vistas, Washington, DC

About the Editors

'Dimeji R. Togunde, Ph.D. is professor of international studies and vice provost for global education at the Gordon-Zeto Center for Global Education, Spelman College, Atlanta, Georgia, USA, where he is responsible for building/strengthening strategic international partnerships aimed at enhancing student international exchanges, faculty and students' research, and students' global learning experiences. Reporting directly to the provost, he oversees the Office of Semester Study Abroad, Cultural Orientation program, G-STEM Program, International Affairs Center, International Student Services and Programming, and all study abroad programs directed by faculty and staff. He directs the operations of the Gordon-Zeto Center for Global Education and stewards a $17 million endowment to support the Campus international initiatives. Dr. Togunde also leads the assessment of the College's internationalization initiatives and collaborates with academic departments to encourage greater awareness of and involvement with the realities of globalization through internationalization of the curriculum and support for speakers on topics of global significance. He has more than 20 years of leadership experience and expertise in developing and implementing global studies curriculum, student learning outcomes, faculty development, accreditation, and strategic initiatives for enhancing access, diversity, and inclusion in international education.

A thought leader and scholar-practitioner in international education, Professor Togunde routinely presents papers and serves as convener/chair of several sessions at many international education annual conferences, including Forum on Study Abroad, NAFSA: The Association of International Educators, Diversity Abroad Global Inclusion Annual Conferences and AIEA (Association of International Education Administrators). Dr. Togunde also serves as an advisor and consultant to several international organizations and sits on Global Studies Advisory Board, Atlanta Global Studies Center External Advisory Board, CEA-CAPA (The Global Education Network) Academic Advisory Board, The Institute for the International Education of Students (IES Abroad) Academic Council, Japan-US Friendship Commission Committee Advisory Board on Diversity, Equity and Inclusion (DEI), Program Steering Committee for Japan Summer Institute, and on the Board of Directors of the International Student Exchange (ISEP) Study Abroad. Previously, he served on the advisory boards of Diversity Abroad Network, The Institute for Study Abroad (IFSA) National Executive Committee

(NAC) Advisory Board and Diversity & Democracy, a publication of AAC&U. Dr. Togunde is a member of Spelman College's Leadership Council.

Previously, he held the John S. Ludington Trustees' Endowed Chair in the Social Sciences; served as Professor of Sociology and chair of global studies curriculum at Albion College, Michigan, where he spent fifteen years before joining Spelman in 2011 as the founding dean of the Gordon-Zeto Center for Global Education. He received his B.Sc. and M.Sc. degrees in Demography & Social Statistics from the Obafemi Awolowo University, Ile-Ife, Nigeria, and a Ph.D. Degree in Development Sociology from Cornell University, Ithaca, NY, USA.

Krishna Bista, EdD, is a Professor of Higher Education in the Department of Advanced Studies, Leadership and Policy at Morgan State University, Maryland. Dr. Bista is the founding editor of the *Journal of International Students*, a quarterly publication in international education. He is also the founding chair of the Study Abroad and International Students SIG at the Comparative and International Education Society. His latest books are *Inequalities in Study Abroad and Student Mobility,* w/Kommers, (Routledge, 2021), *Higher Education in Nepal,* w/Sharma and Raby (Routledge, 2020), and *Global Perspectives on International Experiences in Higher Education* (Routledge, 2019).

Contents

About the Book
Overview of Global Engagement at Spelman
Acknowledgements

1.	Academic Tourist, World Citizen, or Global Ethnic?	1
	Kathleen Phillips Lewis	
2.	Home is Where You Find Your Voice	5
	Fatemeh Shafiei	
3.	Shape-Shifting the Global	11
	Pushpa Parekh	
4.	Give Your Dreams the Wings to Soar	15
	Yan Xu	
5.	Life Changing Experience	20
	Tinaz Pavri	
6.	Walking Back Home	23
	Fernando Esquivel-Suárez	
7.	Living and Working in the Global Community	26
	Alix Pierre	
8.	A Black Feminist Anthropologist Rejects on her Journeys to Brazil	30
	Erica Lorraine Williams	
9.	In Two Weeks' Time	35
	Karen Brakke	
10.	A Momentous Sojourn to Ghana	38
	Dorian Brown Crosby	
11.	The Silver Lining of the Pandemic for Internationalization	43
	Unislawa Williams	

12.	When the Professor Learns *Andrea D. Lewis*	47
13.	Wuothi Eka IneeU *Catherine Odari*	52
14.	Exposure *Margery A. Ganz*	56
15.	Global Travel Experience *Sallie C. Burns*	60
16.	Study Travel as an Extension of a Familiar Place *Rosalind Gregory-Bass*	65
17.	Japan *Chanelle Cunningham*	71
18.	My Experience as an International Student in the United States *Delvonae Beckles*	74
19.	Was it Worth Flying 21 Hours and 25 Minutes *Diane Ingabire*	77
20.	Brown Girl Meets World *Gretchen Cook-Anderson*	81
21.	Wanderlust *Courtney C. Cox*	84
22.	Studying Abroad in Jamaica *Dionne C. Griths*	87
23.	Coming From Japan *Anetha Evans*	91
24.	The Spiritual Path to Spain *Christa E. Sanders*	96
25.	Where I'm From *Keshia Abraham*	101
26.	Like You *Avi Walker*	105
27.	An Experience of a Lifetime *Angelle Cooper*	101
28.	My Tavel Legacy *Kathryn R. Dungy*	112

29.	Unexpected Favor *Mercedes Harris*	117
30.	A Journey of Connectedness through Study Abroad Experiences *Virginia Davis Floyd*	121
31.	From Crowdfunding to a Gilman Scholar and Beyond *Aaliyah J. Deggs*	125
32.	That the Way of the World *Naja Grasty*	128

Chapter One

Academic Tourist, World Citizen, or Global Ethnic?

Kathleen Phillips Lewis

Spelman College, USA

My island home was my oyster, the landscape upon which I found myself. I come from an interstitial place that had its beginnings as a migrant space. It is rare to meet a Caribbean person with no ancestral roots anywhere else but the island where they happened to be born. With the rapid decimation of the indigenous population upon European contact followed by conquest, the Caribbean region became the unwilling host to successive waves of immigrants, both voluntary and forced, melded together to form nations with foreign tastes and ancestral roots in far-flung places. It is also well-known that Caribbean peoples turn their wistful gazes outside to first-world metropolises for vacation travel and seize every opportunity for more permanent outmigration to faraway seductive climes because of a combination of push and pull factors.

EARLY IMAGININGS

While as a child I reveled in the idyllic joys that home had to offer, I nonetheless hungered for the magic of those foreign places my voracious reading had brought to my attention. I embarked on countless imaginary flights of fancy high above and across boundless, fathomless oceans to lands richly endowed with milk, honey, white picket fences and green manicured lawns. However misguided were my early imaginings, they nonetheless gave me an abiding compulsion to script a life writ large with brush strokes that could fill every inch of this expansive canvas that is the world. By the time of his passing when I was eleven, my father had whetted that desire for global travel with his tales of his family's roots in Grenada and Carriacou, his experiences in Egypt and France as a member of the British West India Regiment of the 'Great War for Civilization,' his years working in the gold mines of Venezuela, and his otherwise acquired knowledge of Chimborazo, Cotopaxi, Lake Maracaibo, and other such fascinating geographical wonders of the world. I used to accompany him to his job as an aircraft electrician with British West Indian Airways (BWIA, the forerunner to the current Caribbean Airlines). I enjoyed sinking into the plush upholstered seats of those planes that sat huge and empty in the hangar like so many beached whales. Here I used to pretend I was about to embark on some grand international flight, always destined for a country colder, more developed, and harboring more possibilities, it seemed, than my own.

FIRST ENCOUNTER

When the opportunity finally came for my very first actual trip beyond the shores of home, I was eighteen. It was to the US of A -- a prize trip for winning the National Junior Achievement Secretary of the Year Contest. We formed a contingent to attend the International Junior Achievement Conference on the campus of Indiana University at Bloomington. Yes, I could not otherwise have afforded global travel. When I returned home after that conference and a week stopover in New York, I was a young person inspired -- by what I had seen and sensed, by the friendships I had made, and by my new awareness of how little people knew even in these resource-rich first-world countries about the world beyond their immediate and limited spatial frame of reference. I had discovered that the world was so much larger, so much more intriguing than I had ever imagined from my little *'rinconcito del mundo,'* and it was there beckoning me to enrich myself by more and more encounters with all it had to offer. That first trip abroad gave me a new lens with which to negotiate all earthly phenomena and through which to view and analyze all life's experiences.

Culture shock and the intercultural communication divide were real, I had discovered then and continued to realize, with every global foray. I can write tomes about my countless cultural gaffes, but those are tales for another time and space. The cross-cultural connections I established with my age cohorts from other lands were just as real. There existed some 'universals' that we shared in common despite the broad spectrum of deviation in our cultural contexts, accents, ways of knowing and doing. At eighteen, I made a commitment to enrich my global understanding and expand my horizons through pursuing world travel and intercultural education.

WIDENING VISTAS

The benefits of global cross-cultural exchange, I felt, needed to be shared and experienced by all young people in the formative stages of their lives, and possibly be added in a more intentional way to the curriculum. Accordingly, in my teaching position at a private high school for young women ages 11 to 18, the following year, I organized my first summer study abroad trip for students. We traveled to Barbados to learn first-hand about another

Caribbean culture that was in many respects similar yet in others so different from ours. Despite the glitches, the students enjoyed it and blossomed with new understanding. The rest, as they say, is history.

Since that first burgeoning of global interest, I came to see myself both as part of a larger network and system and yet as an entity of lesser significance in the larger scheme of things, one with an identity that is irrevocably bound up with those of other human beings strewn across chronological time and geographical space. My passion for studying history and global cultures grew with each encounter and I came to see them as inextricably intertwined. My conviction explains why, in the absence of formalized study abroad opportunities when I was at college, I was reluctant to earn three degrees from one institution, or in one country. Attending graduate school in Canada was 'study abroad' for me. For my doctoral dissertation in the days before digitization, I had to spend considerable time and resources conducting research in repositories in the UK, who had laid claim to all official records from those countries that fell victim to its colonization.

RACIAL REALIZATIONS

Now, so many decades later, with the experience of having lived in three countries and having traveled to numerous others in four continents since that time, I look back at all my global intercultural encounters as indispensable learning opportunities that enriched my personal and professional path, textured and deepened my perspectives, and made me who I am today. One of the major paradigmatic shifts I have had as a result of my global explorations is my understanding of race. After growing up in a country where racism was articulated in terms of people of African versus Indian, then witnessing the relatively mild Canadian version of racial discrimination, moving to the US South gave me a rude awakening about white racism of a much more deeply entrenched and virulent type – a phenomenon I describe it as being "on a whole different level," quite unimaginable by those who have never had to live in it. I came to understand why global exchange was necessary to broaden the lens of African American students whose only encounters with race were forged in the US. Accordingly, I understand the disillusionment of many of our students when they visit Africa for the first time and are forced to adjust their shattered expectations of being welcomed back home as long-lost but homegrown Africans, or of being regarded as American rather than as Black sisters in Caribbean spaces, or of falling victim to negative stereotypes, superstitions, and taboos surrounding African Americans or African-descended peoples in general, and black women in particular.

CROSS-CULTURAL UNDERSTANDINGS

Our role as educators, I realized, is to prepare our students to be conscious of their own cultural lenses and how that colors their engagement with other peoples and cultures. I developed, directed, and co-directed study abroad programs, served as Director of the African Diaspora and the World program and as Director of Cultural Orientation with the goal in mind to do all in my power to better prepare our students to enter global spaces with more realistic awareness, positionality, and expectations, and better communicate with people from other cultures. I have learned from all of my global intercultural encounters that: every culture is rich and complete in its own right; every initial intercultural communication barrier can be overcome with the right attitude; deep and abiding similarities are right there lurking beneath the surface of differences; one cannot expect to see eye-to-eye with others when looking down on them with disdain, or with a sense of one's superiority; the wisest option is to cherish diversity while steering always steer clear of all appearances of cultural condescension, mimicry, appropriation, or iconoclasm. I have learned the following: never to try to lay claim to insider status nor seek to make others into clones of yourselves; some of the reactions I first ascribe to discrimination may turn out to be the result of natural curiosity. When I am preparing to encounter a new culture, I try to find out all I can about that culture beforehand, being cautious never to enter seeing its people are subjects for academic research, analysis, and theorizing, but seeking to arrive at a point of common acceptance and respect to foster cross-cultural understanding, for mutual benefit, learning, and growth.

TOUR-IST OR GLOBAL ETHNIC

As Jamaica Kincaid pointed out, *"... every native of every place is a potential tourist, and every tourist is a native of somewhere... every native would like a tour."* Every native wants a tour to help them escape the rough realities of their lives if only for a few moments. The only difference between 'the tour-ist' and 'the toured' is that the 'tour-ist' can afford the tours about which 'the toured' can only dream. As I encounter other cultures, I am ever mindful of viewing myself not as a 'tour-ist,' but as a 'global ethnic' a life-long student, a world citizen, seeking to enter into interactions of mutual respect and acceptance that could reach beyond diverse ways of knowing and doing, beyond differences in the external trappings of cultural origin, and identify areas of common concern in the alleviation of which we can foster cross-cultural, mutually beneficial collaborations. I try to prepare the students in my charge to do likewise.

About the Author

Dr. Kathleen Phillips Lewis, is Associate Professor and Chair of the Department of History and also serves as Division Chair of the Humanities at Spelman College, Atlanta, GA. Her primary research interests lie in the area of Caribbean Economic History, Women, and Gender in the folklore, mythology, oral tradition, and literature of the Caribbean. She was born and raised in Trinidad and Tobago. Email: klewis@spelman.edu

Chapter Two

Home is Where You Find Your Voice

Fatemeh Shafiei

Spelman College, USA

"Travel is the Language of Peace"

Mahatma Gandhi

Over four decades ago, I packed my bags and embarked on a study abroad journey to Los Angeles, California. Although it was not my first international trip, it was my first visit to the United States. I understood this trip was going to be different. This was my first study abroad. I planned to obtain a PhD and return to Iran to pursue a career in Iran's foreign service. However, my journey took an unpredictable path and my life trajectory changed. Never did I imagine that the United States would become my home. Reflecting on more than four decades of life is challenging. I have so many stories to tell—not only about the amazing people that I met along the way, but the historic moments that I witnessed. My study abroad has made a major impact on me, and I consider it one of my life's best decisions. The prism that I aquired is indispensable. The story of my study abroad journey intersects and is woven into the colossal changes of the world in the last four decades.

I had mixed feelings about this trip. I was excited at the prospect of my newly found independence, and I was simultaneously petrified at the thought of navigating life in a new world without my family and friends. I had never lived alone. My mind traveled to the imaginative storylines of my first English lesson in the 9th grade about Gulliver's Travels by Jonathan Swift and Gulliver's adventures/misadventures visiting Lilliput and Brobdingnag. I came to America with my set of values, beliefs, and assumptions about America, American society, and Americans. America's global dominance in the entertainment industry has already influenced popular culture in Iran. Therefore, before coming to America, I was very familiar with American T.V. shows, pop music and movies, but encountering America face-to-face was an entirely different experience. While I brought a detailed map of Los Angeles, pinpointing its different locations and topography, I had no roadmap for the rich diversity of life experiences/encounters that the journey would take me.

Arriving in America

My Pan Am flight from London to Los Angeles was delayed and eventually canceled. The airline booked us on various flights to Los Angeles and as such, my friend in Los Angeles was unable to get my flight information. When I arrived at the airport at 2:00 am, I found that my friend was not there. I was petrified and did not know what to do. Not knowing her address, I decided to go to a hotel. Throughout the ride, I kept remembering my dad's warning that the United States in general and Los Angeles in particular, was not a very safe place for a single young girl. Soon, I arrived at the hotel safely. After that, I decided to take Maya Angelou's advice embedded in her poem, "Do not be wedded forever to fear, yoked eternally to brutishness." This was my first experience of letting my crippling fear of the unknown wither away and strengthen my self-confidence. Moving forward, I decided that I would not capitulate and live my life in fear.

Once at the hotel, I had to call my family and tell them that I had arrived safely. The pace of tectonic shift in communication has been stunning. It must be hard to imagine that there was no smart phone then. I know that in the age of smartphones, it is hard to imagine that at that time calling overseas, especially a non-European country, was quite a challenge. I finally succeeded and called my family and assured them that I had arrived safely and all was well.

Learning to appreciate and celebrate the differences

As a young, sheltered Iranian woman, my perception of the world was confined and shaped by a narrow circle of family and friends who taught me what was right or wrong. As I navigated my life beyond this narrow confine and ventured into new places and connected with more people, I gradually found myself looking at the world from the kaleidoscope of my encounters and seeing its changing patterns that created a colorful path to self-discovery that transformed my life. To my delight, I found that the United States is a much more open society than where I came from. Studying in the United States allowed me the opportunity to broaden my horizon through meeting people from other countries and learning the diversity of life experiences of the world. At the university student housing, I met, interacted, and befriended not only American students, but also students from different parts of the world (Egypt, Japan, Jordan, Russia, South Africa, South Korea, and Taiwan); people I would have never otherwise had a chance to get to know and become life-long friends with.

I discovered that we shared common humanity beneath the cover of cultural and language differences. I learned that what binds us is much stronger than what divides us. I firmly believe that international educational exchange is a catalyst in building bridges to bring people together, debunks stereotypes and discourses of heightened differences, and elucidates differences in a way that forges the strongest possible ties. One learns that "It is not our differences that divide us. It is our inability to recognize, accept, and celebrate those differences," as Audre Lorde states.

Journey to self-discovery

Since I was a child, I was curious about how others would literally see the world. I thought the color of one's eyes would influence how she would see the world. I assumed that people with blue eyes would see everything bluish and the ones with green eyes would see everything greenish. It was not until elementary school that I learned that my assumption was completely wrong about the relationship between eye color and the world one sees. However, only decades later did I learn that the prism that people use in seeing the world is invisible and embedded in their values and not their eyes.

I discovered that identity is shaped more by experience than by genealogy. In turn, my experience was shaped along my gender, ethnicity, class, and culture. Studying in the United States provided intercultural experiences that helped me to understand myself better. The comparative analysis that one engages in from the moment one steps into a new space not only helps in learning a new culture but also helps gaining insight about oneself. Living in a new space puts you in a constant state of comparative analysis and deep diving in the new surroundings, and in the process, you learn, grow, and change. Meeting other people taught me about myself. It changed me in ways that I would never have imagined. Critical thinking and comparative analysis become an integral part of the journey and require you to synthesize and integrate your daily encounters. You digest and evaluate the familiar and not-so-familiar. Your experience pushes you to rethink some of your assumptions and positions about personal and social values.

Studying abroad entails more than just visiting a foreign country to study, but rather provides an unprecedented opportunity to dispel stereotypes, prejudice, and cannon vision that are rife across the world and are fueling racial, religious, and cultural tensions and divisions. It is profoundly transformative. Cross-cultural learning provides a window to understanding a different way of life. Change started to bud, grow, and was nurtured through different encounters both positive and negative encounters, leading me to question "known" and interrogate it as "unknown" in search of a world anew.

Enjoying Freedom in New Home

One of the most cherished attributes of my new home, America, was freedom of speech and press. It is hard to imagine that in many parts of the world to this day these rights are still denied. I love books and the fact that I can read any book without fear of prosecution is priceless. I also appreciate, and tend not to take it for granted, my rights as a woman. I also know more needs to be achieved.

Gender Identity

I was born in Iran. As I reflect on my childhood, I remember that my parents wanted all of their children to get a good education and obtain a terminal degree. However, I was raised to feel equal with my brothers, the society ingrained in me the limitation of my gender. As a girl, I was sorely aware of what it meant to be female and conscious that pursuit of higher education for girls was a privilege and not a guaranteed right. I was the first girl in my family to be allowed to study abroad. Iran was changing and everything was changing for women.

I left Iran before the 1979 revolution, when Iran was at its peak. Through education and participation in the workforce Iranian women's role was changing. I was part of a generation of young Iranian women who were made to believe that women can excel and achieve whatever they set their minds into. Under the law, women were equal to men, though de facto gender bias and discrimination against women were still very much present, yet it was starting to change. When I left Iran, women had the right to divorce and had custody rights over their children. Polygamy was illegal. Women could dress as they desired and hijab was not compulsory. Women could study in co-ed colleges and universities. Women could vote, run, and be elected for parliament, and serve as judges or ministers. The Minister of education at the time was a woman. Not long after the 1979 revolution that overthrew the monarchy, "gender" based apartheid policies gradually yet decisively crept in and were codified into law. Women are now designated as second-class citizens. Women are forbidden to serve as judges and their rights to divorce and custody of their children are among the rights that were stripped away. Women were literally and figuratively relegated to seats in the back of buses.

Years later, as a graduate student in the United States, I was asked to participate in a survey about gender bias in my department. The gender bias inquiry was initiated as a response to a female faculty complaint. At the time, I was gender myopic and did not even know it. I even considered the ability to get higher education as a privilege and not as a right. So, my bar for gender parity was influenced by my socialization and thus was very low. My gender myopia affected my responses to the survey, therefore denying the existence of gender bias in the department. However, later on, I changed and became educated and acquired gender literacy and a new gender consciousness. To this day, when I look back, I regret my responses to the survey.

Spelman Journey

The hallmark of my journey was coming to Spelman College, the vibrant hub of scholarship on civil rights and black feminist thought. I remember, as a young girl, I heard the intellectuals in my family talk and praise Dr. Martin Luther King Jr.'s leadership in advancing civil rights in the United States and beyond. I witnessed the disappointment, the heartbreak, and the mourning that followed his assassination. Coming to Spelman and sitting in the beautiful Sisters Chapel, where Dr. Martin Luther King Jr.'s body lay in rest was surreal.

It was a time of high hope and ominous events. I came to Spelman at a historical moment, when the College for the first-time welcomed Dr. Johnnetta Cole, its first black woman president. It was also the time that police brutality toward a black man, Rodney King, for the first time was captured on film. It was also a time that the nation heard, and many dismissed Professor Anita Hill's testimony.

As I reflect with gratitude on my almost three decades of service as a faculty member at Spelman, I am proud to state that Spelman transformed my life. At Sisters Chapel I heard, learned, and was inspired by voices from thought-provoking progressive and visionary leaders, acclaimed poets and writers, and activists. I witnessed Spelman's enduring legacy of transforming lives through nurturing intellect, building self-confidence, and cultivating a culture of service and civic engagement. Spelman's messages were almost in unison: find your voice, raise your voice, make your voice count, lift as you stand and climb.

The Concept of "Home" Gradually Gets Fluid

I consider the United States my home. You discover that home is not where you are born but is where you find your voice. After living in the United States for more than four decades, and as I struggle to forge my identity, I encounter an everlasting dilemma. As an immigrant I am still often perceived as "foreigner." After hearing my accent, most people still ask me, "where is home?" Although I know that most people don't intend the question to be denigrating, but I find the recent backlash that has sowed mistrust and fear about immigrants alarming. It is alienating to be made to feel like an intruder in your own home!

Conclusion

Globalization created a "global village", but we need to unleash the power of the pulpit of intercultural exchanges to foster compassion and understanding in the village. Mahatma Gandhi, who devoted his life to advancing the rights and dignity of all people, declares that "Travel is the language of peace," and I wholeheartedly agree and add that global education in this "village" is where we encounter, explore, learn, and grow. The intermesh of gender, ethnicity, and political climate pretty much shaped and defined my experience in my new world. Although I came to the United States to obtain a terminal degree, I learned that in the process of getting my degree I grew and changed in more ways than I anticipated. I discovered that intercultural exchanges help to bridge the cultural divide and misunderstanding in the "village" that comes with it. I learned that people are not different in their humanity and their desire and hope for a better world. I discovered that cross-cultural encounter has the power to bridge the cultural, racial, and religious division as it creates unprecedented opportunity to share and understand each other's life stories and aids in building compassion for others. Sifting through my mind and recounting some of the highs and lows of my international experience, I recognize that the rhetoric and discourse about our differences are highly exaggerated. I also realized that the pathway to embracing differences is through conquering the phobia of cultural stereotypes. Harnessing the forces of intercultural understanding embedded in international education is a great asset in advancing peace. Intercultural experience affirms humankind's common bond. Nothing is as transformative as waging global peace by advancing global education in the world.

About the Author

Fatemeh Shafiei is the Director of Environmental Studies and an associate professor in the Department of Political Science at Spelman College. Her research and teaching interests are in international relations, environmental policy, environmental justice, and environmental education. Email: fshafiei@spelman.edu

Chapter Three

Shape-Shifting the Global

Pushpa Parekh

Spelman College, USA

>Shifting sands...
>
>Landscapes across spaces
>
>Choreography of timelessness
>
>Myths unscripted, unhoused
>
>Living in a brutal borderland
>
>Inhabiting a cataclysm
>
>Transforming, filtering
>
>Grains of self...
>
>A dune, an oasis,
>
>Perhaps a mirage...
>
>We are all and nothing
>
>Stories of life and death.
>
>(a poem by Pushpa Parekh)

My Journey

In the nature of explorations, I will share with you my experiences of and reflections on my global journeys that, in the tropes of crossings and cartographies, tell my unique and some not-so unique mappings. Inhabiting and transgressing the borders of my multiple diaspora homes as a migrant of Indian (South Asia) descent, traversing the globe and residing in the U.S for the last forty years, I have learnt that the fluidity and intersectionality of identity markers shape the

contours of my personal and professional life trajectories. As a child of post-independent India, I carry with me in conscious and unconscious ways, its tangled histories, diverse cultures, street vibrancy and shadowlands of multiple colonizations, struggles and persistent resistances. I will give glimpses into how journeying this complex terrain has led me to many place on and off the

codified map grids. My rough approximations of self and evolving identities are simultaneously inter-related and contested, evolving and fluid, yet tangibly located in the body-mind complex. For me, literature has been the life-saving mask against the pandemics of human ignorance and violence, well before the Covid-19, yet urgently felt in the sudden explosion of infections and deaths in India, Africa, the U.S and all over our planet. Somehow, we were knitted by loss and pain, yet we were also witnessing rising racism, nationalism, authoritarianism and distrust.

News and social media images of the dying, hospital shortages, lockdown chronicles, staggering duties of the front-line workers, the unemployed, the displaced migrants and refugees, the portent of climate change effects filled our eyes, crowding our vision with planetary disasters. We also recovered, in the midst of Covid spectre, our hopes in resistance, protests, acts of kindness and self-care.

For me, the Black Lives Matter (BLM) and Me Too protests and movements in the US interlaced with the anti-CAA (Citizenship Amendment Act) and Farmers protests in India. These inter-connections emphasize social justice and human rights demands in the context of police brutality against Blacks in the US (eg. in the wake of Floyd's death) and Indian police arrests of aggrieved Jamia Milla students and Shaheen Bagh protesters in Delhi, India. Anti-capitalist protests by BLM activists and the Farmers' Protests in Punjab, India, are other convergences of note. The year of travel bans and isolation, of political, social and economic set-backs worldwide, has been particularly challenging but also salubrious for mental journeys, psychological stock-taking, and re-imagining a post-Covid world that is more just, inclusive and earth-saving!

He was also obviously a bit pro-Anglo biased when it came to education, though otherwise he spent every evening in the Gandhi library and did yoga asanas each morning. Growing up in an urban North Indian city, Chandigarh, I had in some senses two or more worlds coming together. Known as "the city beautiful" and built by the French architect, le Corbusier, Chandigarh claimed to be "cleaner" than most Indian cities and exuded a sense of order and form (grid like city plan with sectors and house numbers instead of street addresses that had house names or intersecting identifying markers). The city had its transgressive spaces which had the tendency to turn the order and form into a fervor for colorful sights and flavors so abundant in most Indian cities: the chatwallah corners, the busy riksha stands near posh shopping centers, breathtaking Rose garden with Shivalik mountains in the backdrop. In post independent India, Chandigarh occupied an interesting political designation as an "Union territory," sought by both the states of Punjab and Haryana. That meant language issue was always being contested; the resources of water and electricity were never settled; further, being in the middle, meant Chandigarh was culturally a hybrid space. Situated close to the army cantonement base in Ambala, Chandigarh was one of the possible bombing targets during India's war with Pakistan in the '70's. I remember the loud sirens and the smell of the shelter trenches, the sky full of fighter planes on their raid drills, the dark nights with light outs, the sound of anti-aircraft guns as vividly as if it all happened yesterday. All this to say, my life in India was quite a mix of things.

And so it is now. Coming to the U.S, I encountered the race/ethnicity dimension of difference in ways I had never before. I have come to place myself in various categories that I had not even heard of in India, the strangest to me being "East Indian." Today, in the context of claiming diaspora identities, I am often referred to as South Asian. I am proud to be of South Indian origin, with darker skin tone, but also cherish the spectrum of regional Indian cultures, languages and foods: a syncretic, I believe in the various weavings of ethnicities and palettes of human diversity. I went to LSU in Baton Rouge in the early '80's and saw that many students tended to keep to their ethnic groups for the most part. I saw Indians in most Computer Science, Math and Physics departments and very few in Humanities. I loved gumbo and jambalaya and when I could have it, the Beignets were heavenly food! I married and moved to California (both Southern and Northern) to teach in different colleges, and finally settled in Atlanta, teaching at a distinguished Historically Black Women's College, Spelman. My journey has been circuitous, criss-crossing the landscape of outer and inner geographies. When I teach, when I research, when I write, when I speak, I feel myself inhabiting many territories and the spaces between them at times. At other times, I am always at the margins of all territories, finely balancing the privileges and the penalties of being positioned so.

Let me share with you my experiences of teaching and researching as integral parts of my sense of self-community nexus that integrate intersectional discourses and concepts of being and becoming. I teach and research Literatures from 19th and 20th century Britain and Postcolonial/Decolonial Literature Studies with a special focus on Comparative Literatures of South Asia and Africa and their Diasporas. I also study and teach the topics of comparative migrations and diasporas, translocations, displacements and emplacements of post independent subjects of former colonies in the context of globalization and neo-imperialism. As a faculty member, I have engaged with these topics in English and African Diaspora and the World courses. I am deeply interested in connecting with my students and their passion for learning about the local and the global. My lived experiences of being a transnational inform my career, intellectual and affective engagements. I love to travel and have presented academic papers and poetry readings in the US and at various international venues, including Ireland, Canada, Senegal, Morocco, Egypt, Greece, Italy, Jamaica, India, England, Spain and Portugal. I am animated by the crossroads that connect and traverse various mappings of our collective selves and our circles of communities. I believe, as humans we are so much closer than apart. By traveling, I map our human linkages and find resonances in the beautiful diversity of our inner and outer landscapes.

About the Author

Pushpa Parekh, Professor of English and Director of African Diaspora and the World, at Spelman College, is an award winning poet, professor and scholar. Recipient of the 2021 Elite Writers Status by the Poetry Yearbook, Poetry Publications International; the 2019 Gerard Manley Hopkins award; the 2016 West Coast Tagore Festival prize by West Coast Tagore Society, Vancouver, Canada, Dr. Parekh has also published three scholarly books on diaspora and migration topics.

Chapter Four

Give Your Dreams the Wings to Soar

A Cross-Cultural Story of a Chinese Immigrant Scholar-Practitioner at Spelman College

Yan Xu

Spelman College, USA

On a starry summer night in 2005, I arrived in America---the Land of Dreams, after a 14 hours' sojourn from Shanghai, China. It was my first experience traveling internationally. My goal was to pursue a Ph.D. in History from The Ohio State University.

While sitting on the airplane, I felt like a bird soaring through the sky. Interestingly, my first name Yan means a swallow bird in English. My parents chose this name because they wanted me to be blessed with wings of courage, to fly high and pursue my dreams. They had never thought that one day I would fly so far away from them --- 9,320 miles, 3.5 times the distance from D.C. to L.A.

My name fully encompasses my nature. In fact, my friends often compare me to a swallow—easy-going, lovable, and persistently cheerful. But as a historian, I know the connotations of a swallow vary widely across cultural backgrounds. For the ancient Greeks, this bird represents their goddess of love, namely, Aphrodite. For modern Christians, this bird means rebirth or new beginnings. As for me, it symbolizes embracing and adapting to change.

Accordingly, the very first thing I realized was that I was living in a culture very different from my own and I needed to adapt to it. During my first month in America, I regularly fell ill due to drinking cold water after dining outside. I am accustomed to imbibing hot/warm water rather than cold, as is typical in China. Also, in my culture, food is vital to any gathering as it has the symbolic meaning of expressing and establishing relationships between people and their environment. For example, a Chinese hotpot, more of a bonding experience with loved ones than a dish, is both a visual and metaphoric symbol of harmony and community. The Chinese culture also appreciates food as a work of art that has diversified color, aromatic flavor, and excellent taste as its main features. But when I was invited to my American friend's apartment for a party, I felt surprised to see that only soda and finger snacks were served. Everyone was just standing, chatting, and laughing. I was very hungry that evening, but I still enjoyed it. More importantly, I realized from this experience that informal gatherings focused on small talk and developing relationships was a convenient way to make new connections and adapt to a new culture. There were many other miniature culture shocks that I experienced while studying at OSU. But throughout, the fruitful connections I developed, be it with professors, colleagues, or friends, Americans or internationals – provided me with a tremendous amount of support and comfort. They played a strong role in empowering me with the strength to matriculate through 8 years of study, culminating in my Ph.D.

As much as my connections were invaluable to my personal and professional growth, my first years in America as an international student also taught me that it was okay to be different. Later on, my experience at Spelman College imparted upon me the knowledge that being different was not just okay, but something to be thankful for. Having an "outsider" perspective presents unique ways to contribute to the group and develop myself.

Fast forward my timeline to 2014. It was another starry night, when I arrived at my apartment in Atlanta, Georgia. Rather than flying, I drove 637 miles from D.C., where I taught part-time at The Catholic University of America. Different from my flight from China to the U.S. 9 years ago, this time I was traveling with my two daughters --- 5 years and 3 months old, respectively. I was excited to join Spelman – a global leader in educating and empowering women of color – as an assistant professor of History. My excitement was beyond the job itself. I was ecstatic for the opportunity, to immerse myself into a proud community where I could learn and contribute.

I flourished within the Department of History and the Division of Humanities, where I had the pleasure to work with wonderful teacher-scholars from around the world. I worked with colleagues in the Asian Studies Program Committee and Spelman's institutional partners to support Black women in becoming specialists in the field of Asian Studies. Further, I grew in my affiliation with the Gordon Zeto Center, where my team made possible students' dreams of studying abroad in China. These experiences increased my cultural metacognition and taught me to collaborate with diverse colleagues. From day one, I was honored to be part of the Spelman family. And over time, I came to think of Spelman as my second home.

Believe it or not, my sense of belonging at Spelman was most reinforced by none other than the students themselves. In the summer of 2019, I led 8 Spelman girls to study abroad at Heilongjiang University in China's Ice City Harbin. We spent a total of 4 weeks together, day and night, attending Chinese language and culture classes, dining at the school cafeteria, shopping for knick-knacks at the night market next to the campus, and taking mini-excursions by bus on the weekends. In our last week together, we all took a train to Beijing, China's capital. Our group climbed to the top of the tourist area known as "Lakeside Great Wall." While appreciating the breathless scenery, we proudly sang Spelman College's theme song, "A Choice to Change the World." As our singing echoed in the mountains, I realized that the passion for making a difference in the world was what connected me to the students, no matter our unique backgroundsor walks of life. A few students shared with me their life stories as first-generation college students or as work-study students. But one question stood out: "Does skin color define someone as a person?" To me, asking me this question meant that students considered me as someone they trusted. I replied: "Skin color does not define you as a person. Give your dreams wings to fly. Whoever tells you otherwise is telling you a lie."

Any person, no matter who they are, has the potential to change the world for good. But part of changing the world involves being a committed lifelong learner. To that point, I am reminded of the time back in August 2020 when I had the honor to introduce Professor Nell Irvin Painter as the distinguished guest speaker at Spelman's annual Faculty Institute meeting. Professor Painter, a leading historian of the U.S., is the Edwards Professor of American History, Emerita, at Princeton University. Instead of resting on her laurels, she surprised everyone in her life by deciding to return to school after retiring and finally pursuing her lifelong love of art.

Professor Painter's speech of self-reinvention at the meeting could not come at a more opportune time. The year 2020 is noted for being a period of global strife; a raging COVID-19 pandemic and a fever pitch rise in racial discrimination, challenged our society in many ways. Her speech inspired me to go beyond adapting to change—it pushed me to take even greater initiative to become a change agent myself. As such, I actively strived to make changes to improve myself every day. For instance, to improve my program leadership skills as the Chairwoman for the History Department, I stepped outside of my comfort zone and learned the project management discipline. Consequently, I became a successful certified Project Management Professional (PMP).

I have gained through my training in History, project management, and program leadership, a new identity as a scholar-practitioner. In the summer of 2021, I began serving as the Vice President of Professional Development in the Project Management Institute (PMI) Silver Spring chapter. I also developed two courses for Spelman's Project Management Certificate Program with the support of Associate Vice President eSpelman Operations Dr. Tiffany Watson and senior instructional designer Judy Tseng from Spelman's partner Collegis Education. I am most recently so humbled and honored to be involved in the building of eSpelman, Spelman College's new initiative that provides flexible upskilling certificate programs for working adult learners. With my new role as eSpelman Online Program Director, I am thrilled to encourage and support working adult learners from diverse backgrounds to live on the frontiers of possibilities and make the impossible possible.

In August 2021, Spelman College reopened the campus for in-person teaching after the pandemic broke out in early 2020. On a memorable day in early fall, I was walking on the campus and suddenly felt in awe of how all my experiences, connections, and changes to better myself and the world had ultimately led me here. Here I was, not as an "outsider" as I felt when I first came to America, but as part of a family – the Spelman family. I am contributing my small part to a global leader with a rich tradition of educating and empowering women leaders for over 140 years. As I gazed at the resplendent beauty of the scarlet maple hands and golden leaves of the surrounding foliage, I could not help but smile. There is an energy here, an implacable optimism, a strange mixture of humility and daring. It buzzes with immense vigor as if the ground is pushing you to make a choice to change the world, starting with yourself. My working adult fellows, are you ready to give your dreams the wings to soar?

Standing with my Spelman student Shilonda Johnson on top of the "Lakeside Great Wall" in Beijing, China (June, 2019)

The China study abroad program group posting at Jingshan Park — the Royal Garden to overlook the Forbidden City

About the Author

Yan Xu, Ph.D. PMP, is eSpelman Online Program Director, former Chair of the Department of History, and Associate Professor of History at Spelman College. She developed the eSpelman Project Management Certificate Program, and currently serves as the Vice President of Professional Development at the Project Management Institute Silver Spring Chapter. Email: yxu@spelman.edu

Chapter Five

Life Changing Experience

A Study Abroad that Turned into Forever

Tinaz Pavri

Spelman College, USA

Engaging with our students as they embark on their journeys of discovery overseas, leading study abroad programs all over the world, discovering new cultures and traditions through the eyes of my students (some of whom travel abroad for the very first time), I am often reminded of my own coming to the United States as a graduate student.

Securing a scholarship that enabled me to study Political Science and International Relations, my life-long passions, my journey included painful goodbyes to a large and closely-knit community of family and friends who had lived in the same place all their lives, Bombay. It included the nervousness brought about by a U.S. visa application that was often denied to student applicants from the global South. It included making sure that one made minimal demands on one's family in terms of what one asked for, because the dollar-to-rupee exchange rates were punishingly deterring, and one did not want to place untoward demands on one's family. For me, it also included my large, garrulous extended family and friends all dropping me off at the airport with endless exhortations to study hard, be safe, and above all, come back soon. In those days, travel was not the ubiquitous option that it has now become (prior to Covid 19, of course), and going abroad to study came with the knowledge that you did not know when you would see your closest and dearest family members again.

Going to graduate school in a small city in America was a sea-change from life in an Indian megapolis. Public transportation was hard to come by, and initially, life felt, paradoxically, daunting and limiting at the same time. Daunting, because it was filled with so many new experiences to adjust to; limiting, because it did not offer the same expansive horizons and choices that life in Bombay did – plentiful and cheap transportation, food carts, and a vibrant life playing out on the streets that didn't really ebb until late at night. In the U.S., my first impressions were that there seemed to be hardly anyone around, everyone seemed to retreat to their homes at dark and the streets remained preternaturally quiet.

Of course, these first impressions slowly morphed into the reality of everyday life. We international students got immersed into life in the American academy. The informality of the graduate classroom was a shock to us formally-raised Indians who would never have dreamt of calling our professors by their first names. Although many of us knew English perfectly, American accents were tricky to understand, and the continuous references to sports or pop culture via TV shows took a while to adapt to. Even so, friendships were forged as we supported each other through challenging courses and term-paper deadlines. Some of these friendships became life-long. I even attended some sporting events, although I never got the hang of football or baseball, and they don't compare in any way, in my estimation, to cricket.

Being in the classroom exposed me to a wealth of cutting-edge material in my field that would never have been possible had I stayed in India. I grew to appreciate the back-and-forth of the discussion-based classroom, unlike the lecture-heavy classes in India. Questions were welcome, unlike in the Indian educational system which we were used to. The easy availability of the breadth of literature in my field – journal articles, books, documents, databases – allowed me to test the critical theories dominating my field and stretch the depths of my knowledge. The resources available for graduate students in the library were enormous, and if more were needed, ordering them was possible in a way that could never have been in India.

In the first year, many Indian students from large cities discovered that there was an American city in which they felt completely at home because it was just as diverse, just as bustling, home to excellent public transport, and stayed open until the wee hours. That city, of course, was New York. To me, New York was where I could get a quick antidote against homesickness for Bombay and where I felt free again in a way that a limiting college town did not allow. The sights, sounds, and energy were all familiar. It still remains my most-loved city to this day.

At some point, the U.S. began to feel more familiar, and India farther away. One never stopped missing home, but home began to be America as well, an America that didn't just change us, but that we changed to fit our expectations and cultures as well. There were some things about being in America that India could not replicate – the amazing diversity of the cultures of countless immigrants from hundreds of countries. One realized quickly that this was one of the greatest strengths of living in this country. And in the decades that passed, America became more comfortable as it became more diverse.

In the years since becoming a Spelman professor, I've had the privilege of traveling abroad many times, sometimes reliving my initial coming to America. Some of my visits were to faculty workshops or programs overseas. The initial awkwardness of meeting and working with a completely new group of people sometimes evokes memories of those first lonely weeks as a student in America. On the other hand, in my travels with students, I see the new countries they have selected to study in, through their eyes – the newness, the unknown, their struggles with race and racism, which can be expressed in different but just as hurtful ways in these new places. I applaud them for placing their experiences abroad in the context of their learning back home as they pay special attention to the issues of women's and minority rights, often challenging their host for more profound answers to the problems they see.

I also see their excitement and pleasure at figuring out new traditions and cultures, new ways of doing things. One of the most gratifying things for me is to read their post-trip essays, where they mention the growth that their experiences brought and their surprise at how the most overtly different f countries presented them with several similarities to their own lives – their families, friends, and communities back in the U.S. In the end, that trite observation -- that our world is bound together because of our very humanness - holds true as we travel the globe. If we did not lose sight of this, our world might eschew its depressing cycle of violence and confrontation in favor of a common good for all.

About the Author

Tinaz Pavri is the Division Chair for Social Sciences and Education and Director of the Asian Studies Program at Spelman College. She is a professor of Political Science with expertise in South Asia in general and India in particular.   E-mail: tpavri@spelman.edu

Chapter Six

Walking Back Home

Fernando Esquivel-Suárez

Spelman College, USA

We never took a taxi back home from The Council on International Educational Exchange(CIEE) facilities. We would rather walk for 20 to 30 minutes through Santo Domingo's effervescent streets at dawn. As immigrants from cities of Hispanic urbanism, we yearned for crowded, loud, lively streets. We would take the opportunity to complain about living in cities deprived of sidewalks and public spaces in the United States. We indulged in our pedestrian nostalgia. "Esto es vida!", Julio would say abruptly in the middle of our fast-paced walk and he would spread his arms as if he wanted to embrace at once the laughter of domino players coming out of the colmados, the aroma from the old cafe of the Spanish Civil War refugees, the music blasting from cars stuck in traffic. By the time he brought me along as a co-director of Spelman's study abroad program in the Dominican Republic, Julio was already well known in La Zona Colonial - almost as famous as his favorite character, La Marilyn de Santo Domingo. On our walk through La Zona, many would wave at him and yell from afar... "Queloque gallego!" Others would stop him to catch up, turning our way back into a social event.

The last time we did this talk we were coming back from our farewell dinner. In our program, students, faculty, host families, and staff used to gather at a nice restaurant one last time to celebrate a month of closely living and working together. We really bonded that year. You could tell from the already teary eyes of students and host families "doñas" who knew their time together was about to be up. But the mood was actually very festive. After we finished dinner, the restaurant's in-house merengue band performed, and we all danced and took pictures, exchanged information, and promised we would see each other again. For some, these bonds become life-lasting, and those promises are fulfilled. The students took advantage of our last night in town to go out one last time, and, as usual, Julio and I walked back home.

That night, we went over our itinerary for the next day. Who goes in the first van? What students have late flights? Double-checking everything, Julio being thorough as always. We also discussed how successful the program had been that year, and ruminated on the best moments of our journey. We talked about our field trip to Ingenio Boca de Nigua. The ruins of a sugar mill whose furnace was powered by the labor of enslaved people from Africa during the Spanish colonization. The place is eerie, to say the least. There are nefarious objects including the rusty rings, embedded in the columns, that were used to attach the chains that bonded people. But there is also some beauty to it. We talked about the meaning of the moment when a few students climbed to the top of the ruins and took selfies. How they stood victorious, their long dresses flying in the wind, on top of this icon of oppression and ignominy.

We also remembered the emotional discussion with the filmmaker Daga Gautreau after watching her production, *Tanibol*. This video performance guides the viewer through a multiplicity of Santo Domingo's Black women's experiences including sexual harassment, colorism, and colonizing tourism (#wediewhereyouvacation). The film highlighted the affective resonance in the lives of women in the diaspora which brought many to tears during the QnA. We interrupted our walk to grab a drink at our favorite colmado, and continue the conversation. Our personal favorite excursion, the day-trip to Kalalu monopolized our tête-à-tête. At this Afro Caribbean Cultural Research and Creative Action Lab, located in a small village outside Santo Domingo, Black Dominican young women and girls learn Afro-Caribbean music and culture. Under the guidance of Marily Gallardo and her pupils, Spelman students learned dances of the diaspora that have been preserved in communities and organizations like Kalalu. We played drums and danced to Afro-Dominican rhythms for hours. Fostering a space of mingling for Spelman students and their Dominican peers, our excursion ended with an abundant vegetarian meal prepared by Kalalu's staff. Julio and I could not go back home before recounting our visit to the Batey, as Haitian immigrant communities are known in the Dominican Republic. Spelman students went to the local school and observed first-hand an issue that has puzzled them since they learned about it in our courses on campus: the racially motivated discrimination against Haitians in the Dominican Republic. La Española is an island partitioned by the French and Spanish empires, forming the two countries. The border made the African descendant populations of the island one Spanish-speaking and the other francophone. The rejection of Blackness by many Dominicans - who consider Haitians its embodiment - exacerbate the class, citizenship, and linguistic divisions that separated these two communities of the diaspora.

We finished our drink and took a last stroll around Duarte park in La Zona Colonial. I took advantage of this moment to thank Julio for taking me to the art gallery where he used to acquire art from Haitian and Dominican painters. I wanted to thank him for cultivating my taste by introducing me to the work of maestro Cisneros and the promising Jean Guy. I actually wanted to thank him for more than that. I wanted to tell him that he had also nurtured my leadership skills, that he had made me a better educator, a better traveler, a better person. I wanted him to know the dimension of his impact in my personal life and the lives of students, staff, colleagues, host families, and everybody else who interacted with him. But I didn't. I thought it would have been redundant because somehow he knew. I should have done it.

We went back to the building where we rented the small studios where we used to stay while working in the program. We went over our morning plans one more time, we embraced, and said good night. Half an hour later, I heard the particular squeaky noise his door made. He was going out to breath in one last time the nocturnal air of the city he loved so much.

In loving memory of Julio González-Ruiz

Spelman Students at Kalalu Danza Artes Escenicas. Santo Domingo, May 2019.

About the Author

Fernando Esquivel-Suárez is an Assistant Professor in the Department of English at Spelman College in Atlanta, Georgia. He received an M.A. and a Ph.D. in Latin American Studies from Emory University. His background includes training in cultural studies and philosophy at Universidad Javeriana, in his hometown Bogota – Colombia. He is a former fellow at the National Humanities Center. His main research interests focus on African American/Latinx relations, overlapping oppression, and solidarity in the context of the War on Drugs in Colombia, Mexico, and the United States.

Chapter Seven

Living and Working in the Global Community

Alix Pierre

Spelman College, USA

In March 2020, when then-President Trump announced that the US was suspending all travel from Europe for the next 30 days to keep new Covid-19 cases from entering the country, I was traveling to the island of Guadeloupe with the Miami-based art collective Diaspora Vibe Cultural Arts Incubator (https://dvcai.org). Even though the island is in the Caribbean, as a French overseas department, it is part of the Schengen zone, and the same rules enforced in Europe apply. The federal ban was to take effect on March 13 at midnight. We flew back to Fort Lauderdale the same day hours before the deadline.

The Formative Years: Living In The Global Community

I have been collaborating with DVCAI for 6 years as the scholar-in-residence. The partnership captures the essence of who I am in the world as a human being, citizen, and academic. It is at the core of my being as a world traveler; it informs my research in African Diaspora Studies, and guides my interest in and practice of global education. I am part of the many Americans born outside the US. I was born in Guadeloupe, French West Indies and grew up in Paris, France. I was raised in one of the most multi-ethnic and multi-cultural districts of Paris, the 18th arrondissement. I went to school with students from all over the world including Europe, Africa, Asia, the Near East, Far East, Middle East, and North America. In high school, my best friends and I constituted a model UN of sort: Latifa of Algerian descent, Anne-Marie of Spanish ancestry, Rozel from the US,

Maria of Portuguese background, European French, Isabel, Eric, Sylvie, Françoise and Nathalie, Roger whose parents were from Martinique, Boris of Russian extraction, and Saïda of Tunisian origin. Some years later, I graduated from the Université de la Sorbonne with some of them and the new friends I made at the undergraduate and graduate level that completed the world map. There was Anne of Senegalese and French ancestry, Sara from Reunion Island, Clarisse from Mali, Patricia from Guadeloupe, Pierre from Togo, Tatiana the Russian, and Leila from Morocco along with Sophie from Toulouse.

I grew up eating French, North African, Asian, Tex-Mex food, and other culinary delicacies. I tried those dishes at my friends', at home or while traveling. I see myself as a cultural bridge builder. That is why when six years ago the art incubator called, I answered.

Researching The Diaspora

DVCAI was founded by Rosie Gordon-Wallace in 1996. The art incubator has twenty-six years of practice in intercultural art competency across the Black Atlantic. As such, it is conversant in contemporary transnational Diasporan art and cultural identities.

With its headquarters in Miami, Florida, the incubator comprises creatives living and working in the US. Whether born or raised in the United States, those culturally hyphenated citizens confirm the irreversible demographic trend which characterizes the population in this country: it is more diverse than ever. An equally important part of DVCAI's pool of artists resides and works in the Caribbean, Latin America, South America, and Central America.

Traveling with the DVCAI artists during our International Cultural Exchanges, facilitating artist talks, round tables, workshops, coordinating studio visits, and the collaborative exhibit where we constantly engage artists, art lovers, and art and culture professionals in the host countries have afforded me some invaluable insight into transnational Diaspora living. Besides the art, other memorable moments are those spent tasting the local cuisine. I have vivid memories of the meal prepared by Guadeloupean visual artist Kelly Sinnapah Mary's family. As part of the Guadeloupean East Indian community, they treated us to an amazing chicken curry and rice feast. We ate with our fingers off banana leaves, sitting on the ground with our feet crossed.

Equally unforgettable was our dinner at the *Tuani Garifuna* restaurant in Dangriga, Belize, the heart of Afro Belizean culture. The restaurant owner regaled us with some *Hudut*, a dish consisting of pounded plantain, a heated coconut milk sauce with some fried fish on the side. Overlooking the ocean, the restaurant offered a meal complete with music and a dance performance. Many artists were struck by the resemblance with singing, drumming, and dancing practices common to other Afro-descendants. The Dangrigan musicians were surprised at the dancing skills some of us displayed.

The after-performance conversation reminds me of a talk with the dancers of the prestigious Bale Folclorico da Bahia during the seminar I taught at the invitation of the University State of Bahia. During the 10-day collaboration at their headquarters in the

Pelourhino neighborhood we compared the music traditions of Bahia and Guadeloupe. To conclude the colloquium, I prepared a Guadeloupean meal with fresh produces bought at the Feira da São Joaquim farmers' market. I cooked *Didiko,* the old-style Guadeloupean breakfast that can still be had in the rural areas today.

We reflected on the commonalities of the African-based cooking techniques. The dancers were curious about the retention of African customs among Guadeloupean islanders who are French citizens by birth. I explained that like Afro Brazilians and others Afro descended Guadeloupeans maintained the ritual of pouring a few drops of rum on the ground as a sign of reverence to the ancestors before partaking of *ti punch,* the rum-based national drink.

Infusing The Classroom With The Global World

Since in the ADW program we instituted professor-led conversations where faculty members discuss their research with students, I have presented on my work with DVCAI. My talks have helped students further understand the relevance of topics discussed in class as they apply to the lived realities of Afro descendants.

Additionally, I help further internationalize the curriculum and campus by inviting Afro descendants to my classes. The most recent example is my collaboration with Dr. Maurita Pool, the Clark Atlanta University Art Museum Director and Guadeloupean artist Guy Gabon the recipient of the 2019-2020 Black Optics Artist Residency. My students visited the two exhibits Gabon held in the fall and spring. During the conversations with the artist, I served as an interpreter and translator from French into English and vice versa. Moreover, my classes were assigned Gabon's exhibit for the fall 2020 Museum Audio Narrative project.

Serving The Metro Atlanta Glocal Community

I collaborated with a nonprofit organization, World Relief. They work in the field of refugee resettlement. For three months with two friends, we assisted a family of nine from Central Africa settle in Clarkston. We designed a curriculum that met their needs. We taught them how to apply for a public library card and check out material. We helped them navigate the transit system. Included in the curriculum was also sampling American cuisine. The last unit covered grocery shopping..

Going Global With Spelmanites

Conscious of the benefits students derive from global education, I have co-directed study programs to Peru and Portugal. Additionally, I teach the Global Education Seminar for the Gordon-Zeto Center for Global Education. I designed a cross-listed course on Afropeans to offer students the proper language to discuss contemporary French Afro-descendants. In partnership with a colleague in the department of Art and Visual Culture I co-created a course on contemporary Senegalese culture as part of a summer study abroad program.

Lesson Learned

Through my various global experiences, I have learned the importance of being open, and trying as best as possible to suspend judgment. I have found that two of the most significant people connectors are food and music. You must be willing to try. I don't eat red meat or pork but when I travel, I make it a point to taste whatever is on my plate unless it's life-threatening (I am allergic to fresh carrots). In Canada, I ate beaver and seal meat.

In Senegal, I learned that Islam is not as restrictive as elsewhere. I spent a lot of time interacting with art and craft vendors and many of them were women. I expected them to be veiled and withdrawn. Most didn't wear veils and were outgoing. At times, I had to remind myself that I was dealing with Muslim women. I was reminded that in Africa as well as in the Caribbean, Latin America, South America, and Central America bargaining is an art and way of doing business. Finally, guidebooks, websites, and apps are great but ask the locals if you want the best experience..

About the Author

Alix Pierre is a Senior Lecturer in the African Diaspora and the World Program and Director of Cultural Orientation in the Gordon-Zeto Center for Global Education. His research focuses on the Diasporan retention and transformation of culture that includes the feminist perspective. He favors a transnational approach to Diasporic cultural production(s) beyond the boundaries of nation-states. He explores the representation and visualization of black bodies, voices, thoughts, and aesthetics across media. Since 2015, he has collaborated with the Miami-based Diaspora Vibe Cultural Arts Incubator (DVCAI) as co-project manager and scholar-in-residence. Email: apierre@spelman.edu

Chapter Eight

A Black Feminist Anthropologist Reflects on her Journeys to Brazil

Erica Lorraine Williams

Spelman College, USA

My interest in Brazil was sparked when I attended the Brazilian Independence Day Festival in New York City as a college sophomore. It was there that I saw and heard Samba for the first time. From that moment on, I vowed to learn Portuguese, Samba dancing, and travel to Brazil. It took several years, but I finally made it to Brazil in January 2001 as a participant in the Council on International Educational Exchange (CIEE) program. I spent five weeks in São Paulo studying at the Universidade de São Paulo (USP), and five months in Salvador studying at the Universidade Federal da Bahia (UFBA). Drawing upon my experiences living with homestay families as a student in Brazil, as well as my students' experiences with homestay families that I witnessed as co-director of the Brazil Summer Study Abroad program, this essay emphasizes the importance of having a well-equipped team identify homestay families that are suited to the needs of Black women students.

The Journey to Brazil: Scholarships and Accidents

As a first-generation college student from a low-income family, the first order of business to make my dream of traveling to Brazil come true was to figure out how to pay for it. I won a national scholarship for study abroad, as well as a scholarship from CIEE, but I still had to rely on money saved from my part-time job, as well as a "side hustle" of teaching English classes while in Brazil to make it through the entire period abroad. As luck would have it, I had a car accident shortly before my departure for Brazil. I was visiting my family in Fayetteville, North Carolina. After a long day of doing last-minute errands with my best friend, we were struck by a pickup truck on the passenger side of the car, where I was sitting. The force of the airbag caused lingering pain in my chest, neck, and shoulders for several weeks. My knee slammed into the glove compartment and swelled up to the size of a softball. As the paramedics cut through my favorite pair of patchwork jeans, I laid on the ambulance stretcher thinking - what about my trip to Brazil? In the ER, I had X-rays and received a neck brace. Fortunately, I had no broken bones or significant injuries. When I asked the doctor about my upcoming trip, she said, "You're going to be in pain. So, you can be in pain here or you can be in pain in Brazil." It was an easy choice to make.

Homestay Family Blues

About a week after the car accident, I boarded a Greyhound bus to New York, where I caught the CIEE group flight to São Paulo. My homestay "family" lived in a nice apartment in the centrally-located Vila Olympia neighborhood. I put "family" in quotes because my homestay mother, a sociologist, was away doing fieldwork on the Movimento Sem Terra in Northeast Brazil for the entire length of my stay. As a result, I never even got to meet her! Nonetheless, I stayed in the apartment with her 24- year-old daughter, a white Brazilian woman I call Clara.

I was very unhappy with my homestay experience in São Paulo. Clara rarely cooked and had a very frail, elderly woman who would come a few days a week to cook and clean the apartment. It made me very uncomfortable to see this diminutive elderly woman doing domestic chores in the apartment. One day, Carla went to a wedding and I stayed home to pack my belongings in preparation for my move to Salvador. Nobody had cooked that day or the previous day. There was not even any bread for breakfast! The only thing in the refrigerator was week-old rice and beans. I ended up eating a cucumber and brownies. As my stomach growled all day, I grew even more frustrated when I recalled that homestay families received $600 USD per month to provide room and board for us.

Another African American woman in the study abroad program had a lovely Black family who lived in the neighborhood of Butantã near USP. The family consisted of a mom, dad, and two kids – a boy and a girl, age 4 and 9. One day, she invited me to accompany her and her homestay mom to a Black shopping mall. There were so many Black Brazilians everywhere, there was music blasting and lots of Black hair salons. I felt right at home. I wondered why CIEE had not exposed us to Black neighborhoods or cultural sites in São Paulo, especially since Brazil has the second largest population of African descent outside of the African continent.

There were unexpected challenges I faced in Brazil dealing with culture shock, homesickness, and loneliness. It turned out that eating at McDonald's and watching American movies were my go-to things to deal with being homesick. During the first month in São Paulo, I must have eaten at McDonald's 3 or 4 times! I wrote in my journal about having the "overseas blues" and feeling out of place. I'd imagined myself as strong and independent, but I was starting to question this perception of myself. Why was I feeling depressed in a place I had always longed to visit? To be sure, my injuries from the car accident put a damper on my ability to dance the samba. I was also worried about having enough money to make it through the six months in Brazil. While people often emphasize the adventure and delight of being in a new place in discussions of global travel, what is less often discussed is the loneliness, sadness, and challenging adjustments that also come with global travel.

Finally, Salvador!

On February 20th, I finally arrived in Salvador and met my new homestay family, which consisted of an elderly white Brazilian woman who I will call Veronica, and her two teenage nephews who were from the rural countryside but lived with her part-time to attend school. The apartment was nice and centrally-located in the *bairro nobre* (elite neighborhood) of Graça. On the first morning that I woke up in Salvador, I was struck by the sunlight – by 6am bright rays of sunlight began streaming through the windows. This early morning brightness created a different rhythm to life and the day in Salvador. I am generally not a morning person, but the Salvador sun energized me.

Within the first few days of living in the homestay family, I had begun to make a few disturbing observations. First, Veronica had a Black domestic worker – who I will call Julia - who she always called "girl," while Julia called Veronica *a senhora* - the Portuguese term of respect when speaking to someone older than you. Veronica specifically told me not to use *a senhora* for Julia even though she was my elder, but rather call her by her first name. I wasn't comfortable living in a house where an older white woman yelled orders at a Black woman. One day, Julia told me she only made $R150 per month and she worked five to six days a week at Veronica's house and one day at another house. I noticed that Veronica talked a lot about class. One day when I was so excited to go see an Afro-Brazilian folkloric dance show, she said "*só vão as pessoas sem cultura*"/The only people who go to those types of things are people without culture." This is basically another way of calling people "low-class." While she initially treated me with surface-level politeness, subtle racism sometimes seeped out. For example, she once showed me a picture of a woman and commented, "she is *mais preta* than us, but she's pretty right?" *Mais preta* can be translated as either darker or literally "more Black." This comment shocked me on multiple levels. First, it was as if she thought it was extraordinary that a Black woman could be pretty! Second, it seemed as if she was lumping "us" together in a common racial identity, which was not the case. Although I identify as a Black woman, she and sometimes other Brazilians, did not really see me as Black because of my lighter complexion. Even though she was white (though perhaps with some indigenous ancestry based on her appearance), our skin colors were similar, so there was an "us" in her mind with which I did not identify.

Within a few days of living in Veronica's home, I wasn't sure if I would be able to stay. I had a sinking suspicion that I wouldn't be in her world if I weren't from the US. It was an odd experience being a young Black woman from a working-class background in Brazil. People assumed that I had money because of my American passport. There were countless annoying moments with Veronica. One day at breakfast, Veronica ordered Julia to put milk in my orange juice because it was too acidic. I thought it was just fine. She often made rude comments about what I was or wasn't eating. I also felt like I had no privacy in her home. She always went into my room without knocking. One day, when I got home, her sister was lying on the sofa in my room. Another day, I got home and was in my room for a few minutes, when one of her nephews opened my bedroom door with a towel wrapped around his waist and a newspaper in his hand! He quickly apologized and closed the door. Once, I got to the apartment and Veronica yelled, "Who is it?!" and rolled her eyes when she saw it was me. She often left the "pega-ladrão" (chain-lock) on the door during the day, which seemed to defeat the purpose of giving me a key. When I entered the apartment, she asked me "*já? Você não está saindo de novo*?" as if she didn't want me to be in the house! Then she called me *caseira (*a homebody) because I spent a lot of time at home one day (even though I had gone out every day before that!)

I wished I could have lived with a Black homestay family. However, I soon realized that none of the students in the program had Black homestay families. How could it be so difficult to find Black middle-class families in a city that is approximately 75% Black? By mid-March, I began searching for a room to rent. When Veronica asked me why I was moving, I told her that it would be cheaper. I wanted to leave with no hard feelings, so I didn't want to tell her how uncomfortable I felt in her home. Ultimately, all of the CIEE students ended up moving out of their homestay families' homes once they realized that they would be able to pocket the $600 USD that was being paid to homestay families. We could rent rooms or apartments for much less, and then pocket the rest of the money.

On the Other Side: Co-Directing a Study Abroad Program in Brazil

At Spelman College, I created and co-directed the summer study abroad program in Salvador, Brazil, along with my retired colleague, Dr. Barbara Carter. We partner with Brazil Cultural, an educational organization run by Dr. Javier Escudero, and his wife, Patricia Burgos. For five years, we took eight to fifteen students and spent four to five weeks in Salvador. For the most part, our students have had very positive experiences with their homestay families. This is partly due to the careful and diligent work that Ms. Burgos does as Homestay Coordinator. Students fill out a homestay family questionnaire that provides details and preferences to better assist Ms. Burgos with matching students with families. Not only have they done an excellent job of reaching out to Black middle-class families in Salvador, but they also ensure that their non-Black families are equipped to host Black women students. On the rare occasion that there has been a problem with a student and the homestay family, we effectively intervened in a timely manner to move the student to another family. Several of our students still keep in touch with their homestay families on social media years later!

About the author

Erica Lorraine Williams is an Associate Professor in the Department of Sociology and Anthropology at Spelman College. She has a B.A. in Anthropology and Africana Studies from New York University, and an M.A. and Ph.D. in Cultural Anthropology from Stanford University. She is the author of *Sex Tourism in Bahia: Ambiguous Entanglements* (2013) and co-editor of *The Second Generation of African American Pioneers in Anthropology* (2018). Email: ewilli29@spelman.edu

Chapter Nine

In Two Weeks' Time

Karen Brakke

Spelman College, USA

Two weeks in May. It's so little time. I have accompanied Spelman student groups on short-term study-abroad programs partnering with the Council on International Educational Exchange (CIEE) four times, traveling to Spain, the Dominican Republic, Chile, and Portugal. As I hear each year of our destination and meet the students and faculty colleague who will share the journey, I am excited for the adventure. Then the questions start to stir as I think about the goals of the program to "identify differences and commonalities of two world societies based on political, economic, social and /or cultural values during each study-travel experience"; and "develop a personal definition of cultural engagement that reflects openness to cultural difference"(Spelman College, unpublished document). How can we possibly learn the language, start to understand the culture, or appreciate the history and heritage of a place in just 14 days? How can we experience all the country has to offer when our free time is limited? How, perhaps most importantly for us as program directors, do we develop relationships of trust and support with our students in that time, so that they will have the confidence to explore while still sharing their vulnerabilities with us when needed?

Two weeks in May. It's a lifetime –or so it seems during the first few days of the program. We are jet-lagged, on new ground, and sensing the apprehension that many of the students feel about navigating an unfamiliar place. Suddenly it has become very apparent that we are guests in another land; language, food, and traditions are different from home. Some students have trouble stretching their horizons and don't like the food, the smaller personal boundaries, or the dogs that wander the streets. My advisor evenings are spent hoping students will stay safe and some nights are spent wondering whether everyone made it home from the clubs that they are compelled to visit. The mornings start early, according to Student Time, and we count to make sure everyone is ready for another day. Occasionally one or two feel ill, or homesick, and the caregiving begins. Classes are interesting and we advisors take on the role of learners as well, even though some of us know exactly what the standard exercises (Onion, Iceberg, Glasses, Fishbowl, anyone?) are meant to do. There's racism everywhere we visit; sometimes overt, like the time someone spat at a student's feet or the mall security guard who verbally harassed a student because of her dark skin. Sometimes situations are ambiguous; are people starting at the group of confident, ebullient young American women or are they staring at the Black women who aren't bound by the cultural and historical mores put forth by this society? Some of my saddest travel moments have been spent talking things through with the groups as they confronted the systemic racism in societies that had, they thought, promised a break from everyday life; racism so deeply ingrained that even our instructors did not recognize it. By that first Thursday (is it only Thursday?) everyone is anticipating the weekend when we can indulge in sleeping in or simply being tourists for a few days.

Two weeks in May. It's a wonderful time. By the second week, we have settled in. We have had some relaxing weekend beach time and know our way around the city; where to go for good food and sightseeing, and – among the students -- shopping and clubs. We become comfortable with public transportation and can order a few things in restaurants without reverting to English. By this time we are friends with our hotel hosts and everyone at our classroom site. We all start to see the layers of life, at turns inspiring, troubling, and mundane, in the community we are visiting. Behaviors that seemed odd just a few days ago now become habits. It is especially rewarding to see those of our group who were initially resistant to adapting to new ways now recognize and embrace the opportunity to grow as they learn as much about themselves as they do our host culture. During this last week as well, students often productively channel their frustrations and become educators with our host instructors on how racism can be expressed and identity shaped. Students' conversations with our guest speakers become more reciprocal and nuanced, and it becomes common for me to share a small, affirming nod with my fellow faculty director as we see the students morph into global citizens.

Two weeks in May. It's our time. As we leave – inevitably very early in the morning -- we are ready to return home but there is always a touch of sadness that we are leaving our new friends and our worldly ways. We all appreciate, too, the time we've been given to explore new environments and our responses to them. Students, even after this brief time, start to understand the history and contexts of our host cultures with all the nuances and ambiguities – good and bad – that shape how we have been received. Many of the students, too, go one step further and reflect on the experiences of immigrants to the US, and vow to be more welcoming on our home soil. Personal identities are interrogated and may shift their contours ever so slightly. Once we are home, after we go our separate ways and then reconvene in the fall, there is a bond among us. We who have shared the two-week adventure know a little more about each other not as students or teachers but as individuals. We share the stories that we alone understand through our experience. All of us sense that we have indeed changed just a little because of those two weeks in May.

About the Author

Karen Brakke is a professor in the Department of Psychology and Co-director of the Teaching Resource & Research Center at Spelman College. Her research interests include skill development in infants and young children, the development of narrative identity in emerging adulthood, and the scholarship of teaching and learning. Email: kbrakke@spelman.edu

Chapter Ten

A Momentous Sojourn to Ghana

Dorian Brown Crosby

Spelman College, USA

Since I can remember, I have been intrigued by other cultures. I have always been fascinated by language, cuisine, clothing, art, music, architecture, customs, laws and other ways people collectively identify themselves. That curiosity about cultures led me to my high school, which offered a magnet program in international studies and courses on Middle Eastern culture including learning Arabic. I participated in a traditional Japanese tea ceremony, and I attended classes with a very diverse student body. Later, as a student at Spelman College, I discovered more about other cultures.

I have come full circle now that I am a faculty member in Spelman's Department of Political Science. I watched my phenomenal professors as a student with awe. They were black women with Ph.D.'s in political science who made me feel that I too could earn a doctorate in political science and someday return to Spelman and teach political science. It has been my pleasure to guide students on their academic journeys to explore the world through global travel. I was also privileged to serve as the inaugural Director of Culture Orientation in the Gordon-Zeto Center for Global Education. I prepared students for their trips to various global destinations in this capacity. Preparation occurred in required classes for all students traveling abroad. Every semester, every destination was assigned a number to create class sections. All students traveling to that country met with that section for four required preparation classes. These classes were called Study Travel Seminar 100 or (STS 100). During my three years as Director of Cultural Orientation, I taught 500 students who traveled to various destinations worldwide every semester, every year. As a result, I taught over 700 classes. Implementing the initial STS 100 course for approximately 40 sections, representing 40 different destinations, while teaching and researching, was a formidable task, however, it was invigorating knowing that I was creating curricula to help Spelman students enhance their cultural competencies. Similarly, I learned about other cultures through the students' essays and roundtable discussions upon their returns to the United States.

In addition to our study abroad program, students traveled for two weeks on faculty-led trips, and under numerous programs coordinated and supported by The Council on International Educational Exchange (CIEE). During the Roundtable Discussions upon their return to campus, students in each section shared wonderful stories about their travels with each other. Listing was inspiring. Some of the highlights from their travels included: recognizing African American cultural links with African peoples in the Diaspora, tasting Ceviche in Panama, the satisfaction of conversing in Spanish or French, overcoming their homesickness, discovering how, when and where to exchange their U.S. currency, comparing public transportation systems, and making new friends at exchange universities in Copenhagen and Italy. Although Spelman offered numerous global destinations for student travels, a group of Spelman students had not yet traveled together to Africa for a culturally immersive trip. Ghana was selected because CIEE offered a program there. Thus, in 2014, Dr. Veta Goler and I were selected to accompany the first group of Spelman students on a CIEE sponsored trip to Ghana. How exciting! What an honor! Learning about Ghana was exhilarating!

The culturally immersive two weeks began with our departure from the Hartsfield-Jackson Atlanta airport early in the morning. I was anxious and excited because this was the first time I had traveled outside the country with students and many of them were going abroad for the first time. Once we landed in Accra, our Ghanaian CIEE director arranged transportation that took us to the hostel (low-cost, communal lodging-somewhat like a college dormitory) where the students lived. Dr. Goler and I resided in the hotel only a few feet from them.

Immersing ourselves in the culture began as we walked a few blocks from the hotel to restaurants. Listening to the automobiles, seeing people walking, looking at the gated homes, and eating in the outdoor restaurant spaces filled my senses. Interacting with the hotel staff was immeasurably enjoyable because they told us the best places for shopping and Ghanaina food. I had so many wonderful conversations with the receptionists that I took pictures with them on our last day in the hotel. Leaving was bittersweet. We had become so friendly with them that it felt like I was leaving my family. Many of our conversations occurred as Dr. Goler and I waited for the bus provided by the Ghanaian CIEE staff to the University of Ghana, where students attended their cultural sessions.

Learning to speak Twi— a dialect of the Akan language spoken in southern Ghana— with the students in their daily language sessions was fascinating. The students were so engaged, and practicing with them was fun. I learned that Ghanaian names reflect the day of the week on which they are born. For instance, Abena is the name for a female born on a Tuesday. A male born on a Friday is named Kofi. I also learned how to say good morning, hello and good night in Twi. Their classes also included guest speakers. One of the lectures from a Ghanaian scholar revolved around the history of Africans capturing and delivering other Africans to colonial powers for free labor in their colonies. I listened intently as the Spelman students asked questions. As an African American, I found it intriguing and somewhat disappointing to hear that Ghanaians considered discussing West African leaders' roles in the Transatlantic Slave Trade contentious. In addition to the cultural classes, we had opportunities to explore Ghana.

We enjoyed several cultural excursions. The sights and sounds of the bustling city were balanced by the serenity of the less urbanized areas. In downtown Accra, we were honored to visit the Kwame Nkrumah Memorial Park and Mausoleum. Equally honorable was our outing to the W.E.B. Du Bois Memorial Center for Pan-African Culture. The open market was a sensational place. The artwork was fabulous. It was a treat to watch the artisans create their wooden crafts. We spoke our recently-learned Twi while shopping and haggling with the shop owners, who were primarily women who sold household items like soap, clothing, rugs, fabric, hand-held fans, hand-crafted jewelry, straw baskets, and other trinkets. Looking at the beautiful fabrics led to another highlight of my trip to Ghana: having a dress custom made for myself.

The students, Dr. Goler, and I commented on the gorgeous dresses worn by the Ghanaian assistants working with us from the University of Ghana. One day after we complimented one of the ladies on her dress, she informed us that we could have dresses made in Ghana. We only needed to select the fabric, have our measurements taken, and work with the Ghanaian seamstress to design the dresses. She would have the garments ready for us to try on and purchase in a week. This was fantastic news!

Selecting the fabric and designing my dress and blazer were most enjoyable. I was extremely satisfied to see the completed items a few weeks later. It was an incredible feeling knowing I was returning home with a dress and a jacket made from Ghanaian fabric by a Ghanaian seamstress in Ghana! I also had garments made for my parents and great maternal aunt. My mother, her mother, and her mother were all seamstresses. My family history made this cultural connection through dressmaking overwhelmingly joyous. Yet, as wonderful as this experience was, other encounters pierced my soul.

Walking through the dark, small areas of "slave castles" where captured Africans waited to be sold into slavery on the TransAtlantic Slave Trade was traumatic. I shuddered to think of what my ancestors endured to survive and make my existence possible. I imagined what they might have felt, smelled, heard, and tasted as they anguished over an uncertain future. I also imagined the language mixtures from various ethnic groups that created a language that allowed captured and traded Africans to survive. It was extremely disturbing to know what gender-based violence my female ancestors endured at the pawing hands of white males. Passing through the sacred "Door of No Return" completed the ethereal circle. For me, it represented the portal where captured Africans left their home physically only to return in the hearts of their descendants who walked through it, coming from the other side.

My husband joined me after the students returned to the states. We were able to share an emotional visit to one of the slave castles that had held our ancestors. My god-brother's wife is from Ghana. She arranged for her brother to assist us with further travels into the city of Kumasi. There, we purchased authentic Kente cloth and returned with a video of the weaving process we had watched. I knew that my maternal and paternal family elders would not return to the Motherland of Africa. Therefore, I thought the next best way for them to see our ancestral shores was through my pictures and videos.

Images of the slave castles deeply moved them. They were astonished at the "mobile shopping" occurring in the streets courtesy of women weaving in and out of cars while balancing baskets of food, cell phones, and other goods on their heads. My family elders—all in their 80s and 90s at the time— marveled at the authentic Kente cloth and the video of the artisans creating the textile. They were very grateful for the images and smartphone videos. These elders represent our family's closest connections to our ancestors. They hold the stories behind our New Year's Day traditions that include foods and beliefs from West African traditions. It was evident that so much of their life experiences include words, homeopathic healing remedies, music, carpentry, and other cultural expressions inherited from Ghanaian ancestors. It was very satisfying to know that I helped them make the virtual journey back home!

My adventures in Ghana are vivid memories for me. They mark a time when I grew as a faculty member by supporting students on a trip abroad. My time in Ghana also expanded my knowledge of Ghanaian politics. As a political scientist, I appreciated conversations with Ghana's CIEE staff. For example, one discussion that stands out revolved around the complexities of purchasing land to build homes and the challenges of getting the homes built. Our Ghanian CIEE director explained that there are cultural traditions involving village chiefs authorizing the purchase of land for building new homes. The politics involved in securing that authorization also can be lengthy and financially costly. The trip also deepened my appreciation for Ghana's rich culture.

Eating traditional dishes of Fufu and Red Red reminded me of how many Ghanaian dishes contain foods used in African American cuisine. Red Red (a black-eyed pea recipe) was so delicious that I learned how to make it. It is now a favorite family dish in my African American household.

I have an even stronger appreciation for the strength and faith it took for enslaved Africans to forge a new life in a strange land than I did before making this pilgrimage trip to Ghana. To honor my memories of Ghana, and as a sign of honor for the sacred ground they touched, I have not worn a pair of sandals I wore on the trip since I returned to the United States.

I am a better person because of my trip to Ghana. It taught me patience, calmness, and reinforced my pledge to be a lifelong learner. I am and will always be eternally grateful for my momentous sojourn to Ghana.

About the Author

Dorian Brown Crosby is an Associate Professor of Political Science at Spelman College. Her research focuses on resettled African refugees in the United States' southeastern region, placing her work in multiple contexts: Forced Migration Studies, American Government, Women's Studies, Ethnic and Racial Politics, and International Relations. Email: dcrosby1@spelman.edu

Chapter Eleven

The Silver Lining of the Pandemic for Internationalization

Unislawa Williams

Spelman College, USA

The Gordon-Zeto Center at Spelman College has been a critical conduit to actualizing international collaboration. The funding and programs of the Center help Spelman students and faculty internationalize. In my case, they have allowed me to build my research abroad, grow and broaden my network of international colleagues and collaborators. The Center has also helped me develop and organize digital international exchange opportunities for students. Many, if not most, of these activities would not be possible without the help of the Center.

Internationalization requires creativity and resources; a conduit helping make international collaboration possible has never been more important than now. The scope of the disruption to international travel inflicted by the COVID-19 pandemic would be unthinkable even two years ago. Thanks to the work of the Center, nearly all of my students have had an experience of going abroad prior to the pandemic. In my senior class today, only those students who had studied abroad as freshmen do now.

However, at the end of their senior year, all political science majors will again have an international experience. Thanks to the Center's creative reimagining of what internationalization means, the students will travel on an exchange digitally. Via Zoom, they will all go to Amsterdam to hear a series of lectures tailored to their specific study. The close alignment with their Spelman coursework was not common prior to the pandemic.

Though the uncertainty of the pandemic is still with us, the new normal appears to benefit internationalization in unexpected ways – addressing challenges to international connection we did not appreciate prior to 2019.

INTERNATIONAL COLLABORATION

The Gordon-Zeto Center programs and funding have allowed me to build my research abroad in several ways. The initial funding, along with a grant from the Department of Education Subaward through the Ohio State University's Office of International Affairs, and Center for Slavic and East European Studies sponsored two trips to Poland. I attended a conference ("XXVII Polish Economic Forum") in Krynica-Zdroj, Poland, and I also conducted archival research on nonviolence and international relations in Krakow, Poland in 2017. Even though I am from Poland, my connections were primarily familial; and because my education was mostly in the United States, I lacked a professional network in Poland. The grants allowed me to grow and develop professional contacts.

While still in Krakow, I was invited to give a talk at the oldest and most famous Polish University, the Jagiellonian University. As a result of these initial grants, not only was I able to travel to Poland and build my research, but I was also able to meet other academics and expand my professional network. Subsequently, I was invited to present at two conferences held in Poland. The expenses were fully paid by the conference organizers for one of the events. I was also asked to serve as a moderator and a panel participant. The experience of developing professional contacts and growing collaborations was accumulating. Along with co-authors, I developed a series of publications about international collaboration.

In sum, the Center's seed money played a key role in making the initial and foundational experience possible for me as a researcher and academic. The funding had a lasting and long-standing impact on my career and opened doors for subsequent opportunities.

While internationalization was a worthwhile and needed aspect of my own work, I was not able to translate these experiences into exchange opportunities for my students. In large part for personal reasons, organizing an international exchange has always been a to-do for the future. While this may have been something to look forward to one day prior to the pandemic, COVID-19 led me to rethink this possibility in fundamental and unexpected ways. Little did I know I was about to take my students on an international exchange right in the middle of the pandemic.

INTERNATIONALIZATION IN THE TIME OF THE PANDEMIC

At the time of writing in 2021, we are still experiencing limitations to international travel that would have been unthinkable in 2019. At the same time, our connectivity has been decoupled from physical contact to a large extent. Although we can contact someone far away, it does not mean that we will take the time to do so. Whether the increased connectivity supports internationalization depends on our ability to rethink international exchange.

One imaginative possibility has been virtual exchange. Through virtual exchange, students could experience a short series of lectures delivered by an instructor living and working abroad. The Gordon-Zeto Center provided a list of potential international collaborators to deliver a small lecture series. The lecture series were to be offered inside existing courses as a short one-to-two week module. The topics ranged as did the international locations of the lecturers. The Gordon-Zeto Center helped to coordinate and offered a stipend to the lecturer for developing the series as well as to the host for organizing it. For the host, the stipend was contingent on having the course approved by the curriculum committee.

My students will be going on just such a virtual exchange to Amsterdam. As seniors in a political science research seminar, they will learn how the policy implications of research can be more than an afterthought of a research paper. The lecturer will discuss how her own research builds access to government resources and education for disadvantaged communities. Although students discuss similar topics as political science majors, the discussion is typically focused on the American context. Having a lecturer speak to a topic of discussion the seniors likely encountered but is now in a context of a new country, offers opportunities to learn and grow one's knowledge, as well as challenge existing assumptions. In other words, it comes with many of the benefits of actual travel and exchange. Students are asked to observe how other societies and cultures work and to learn something about themselves in the process.

Experiencing another culture inside a Spelman course would have been nearly prohibitive by the challenges of travel, especially international travel, but now can be directly applied to learning. The growth and development fostered by international experiences may be brought closer to the research context of the classroom; students may be better able to compare and contrast the perspectives as a result. In sum, the benefits of experiencing another culture can become part of the course materials.

Redesigned and improved with a new international twist, the module on policy implications is now approved as part of the regular Spelman course required of all seniors in the Political Science Department and approved by the College's curriculum committee. Because of the way the experience is institutionalized, virtual exchange is likely to become the new normal for students in the Department. In sum, the pandemic era has taught us lessons about international connections that are likely to stick; lessons that students may find valuable and beneficial for years to come.

Though I see internationalization as beneficial on many levels, it can also be difficult organizationally, expansive, time consuming and disruptive to the daily routine. Considering the necessary planning around the travel, a trip overseas has never had a quick turn-around. Although traveling may have been challenging before 2020, it was arguably easier than in any other time in human history. Abruptly, the pandemic closed the door to international travel (at least temporarily) and opened a new door to digitalized connectivity. While travel may have gotten more challenging, internationalization arguably may have never been easier.

About the Author

Unislawa Williams is an associate professor in the Department of Political Science at Spelman College. Her major research interests lie in the area of data science and international relations. Email: uwilliams@spelman.edu

Chapter Twelve

When the Professor Learns

Reflections from Cuba

Andrea D. Lewis

Spelman College, USA

Spelman College students often engage cultures of the world through extended study abroad and shorter study trips sponsored by the College's Gordon-Zeto Center for Global Education. These global opportunities paired with African Diaspora and the World (ADW), a mandatory course for all first-year students, "prepares students to develop a perception of themselves as citizens of a changing and increasingly compressed world, of sharpening the awareness of diverse cultural and historical experiences and of promoting the association between learning and social change." (Spelman College website)

In addition to the ADW course and the prominence of global opportunities on Spelman College's campus, the course Global Education was created to allow participants to broaden their knowledge of schooling worldwide. The course, also approved as a college-wide International Studies elective, examines the historical, cultural, economic, sociological, philosophical, and political understanding of schooling and education globally.

Initially I proposed a study trip to provide a more impactful and personal learning experience in the Global Education course. During my first semester teaching Global Education, Cuba was a country of intrigue, mainly because of its inaccessibility and perceived mystery. As conversations increased about the Cuban Revolution, varied perceptions of then-President Fidel Castro's leadership, the country's positive relationship within the African Diaspora, and Black fugitives receiving political asylum in Cuba, I researched the possibility of taking a group of Spelman students to Havana,

Cuba. While compiling information from the college, I learned there had never been a Spelman-sponsored faculty-led trip to Cuba. We were entering uncharted territory, but a line in the Spelman College's hymn states, "undaunted by the fight." I became undaunted in my quest to take students to Cuba as the restrictions lifted by former President Barack Obama were easing entry into the country. Through many lessons on governmental approval, submitting documents for entry, and preparing students for our adventure, twenty-two of us boarded a charter flight in Miami bound for Havana in December 2015. We were nervous in anticipation of the mysteries of Cuba, however, once we arrived, our trepidations quickly faded as we saw people who resembled us, and we were welcomed with open arms by everyone we encountered.

"Mi Familia" was a phrase that Cubans yelled out during our visits to schools, community centers, and walking through the streets. Although our focus was to examine the country's education system, the experience went far beyond our trip's original intent and magnified our connection to the African Diaspora. For the students, the trip connected to their courses, Global Education and ADW, and brought to life the realization of the effects of the Atlantic Slave trade. We spoke with people who resembled our family members, which reaffirmed that the only factor that separated us from our Afro-Cuban brothers and sisters was the stop on each slave ship.

The visit provided moments of reaffirmation as we experienced life with the people of Cuba. The students' amazement brought me joy. Our first stop in Havana after leaving the airport was Casa de Africa, a museum dedicated to preserving the history of the African Diaspora in Cuba and housing many of former President Fidel Castro's gifts from African leaders. During our museum visit, a personal, powerful moment occurred when the Afro-Cuban dancers invited audience members to dance to the African rhythms. A group of West African visitors danced alongside the Spelman students and Afro-Cuban dancers. It was an in-the-moment, authentic, and accurate representation of the connections between us rooted in our shared African ancestry. It was a beautiful and spontaneous once-in-a-lifetime representation of the diaspora through music and dance.

Throughout the December 2015 trip and subsequent trips in 2016, 2018, and 2019, the student travelers and I received much more than the intended purpose of the study trip. Combining the educational, cultural, and emotional learning from Cuba created the journey of a lifetime for many of the travelers and had positive implications for their future career goals.

In addition to the cultural connections of the four trips, I enjoyed the teaching and experiential learning aspects because it showed students that class does not have to be confined to four walls or technology-centered. Experiential learning refers to the power of experience in learning that often occurs outside of the classroom (Kolb, 2014). Similarly, Keeton and Tate (1978) defined experiential learning as "Learning in which the learner is directly in touch with the realities being studied. It is contrasted with the learner who only reads about, hears about, talks about, or writes about these realities but never comes into contact with them as part of the learning process" (p. 2).

Our daily classes in Cuba were often held on the go and in unconventional spaces. Also, due to the inaccessibility of on-demand wifi in Cuba, students had to rely on pen and paper, talk to each other, critical thinking skills, and learn without access to Internet searches and online libraries. It meant that I could not rely on PowerPoint slides, online resources, or electricity to plug in a laptop.

To prepare students for this unconventional learning experience, they were reminded multiple times via class, emails, group text messages, and informal conversations to download or print readings needed for onsite class discussions. I packed books, hard copy articles, chart paper, post-it notes, and markers. A documentary viewing assignment was assigned as a pre-trip project, and the syllabus detailed our daily learning aligned with site visits.

During long drives to educational and cultural sites, our class was held on the go using the bus's microphone and a strong arm to stay steady on unpaved Cuban streets. At first, students were amused that class was held on a moving bus, but they were engaged and enjoyed the unconventional approach to teaching. After visiting the sites, we returned to the hotel and finished class in a quiet section of the hotel lobby or by the pools. The workers at the front desk and other hotel guests became accustomed to our gatherings, small group break-out sessions, and student engagement. Class by the pool was enjoyable until afternoon rains scattered us into dry places. Learning outside of a traditional classroom and without the reliance on technology fostered more meaningful conversations, engaged more critical thinking skills, and created a learning community that was fluid and always flexible.

Leading four study trips to Cuba was a powerful learning experience. The trips provided memorable moments that reminded students of their intellect, independence, and tenacity. On two trips, we were not prepared for climbing activities. In Havana, we participated in a city climb and had to lift each other as we tackled a fortress in non-climbing shoes and outfits. A particular student who was afraid of heights had no option but to go forward. She broke down in tears, but her Spelman sisters lifted and encouraged her step by step until she reached the top. We were all tired, frustrated, and overwhelmed when we made it to the top of the city mountain. As we entered the last hurdle, we looked up and were face to face with a statue of Jesus that overlooks the city of Havana. While it was not meant to be a religious activity, many saw the parallels between the struggle to climb the city mountain and then coming face to face with Jesus at the top.

On our last pre-pandemic trip to Cuba, I confronted my fear of not being in control. I always needed to know the next step, the next move, the next event. In June 2019, instead of going to metropolitan Havana, we visited the mountainside of Santiago de Cuba. During one of our overnight excursions, the tour guide took us to the Sierra Maestra Mountains to retrace the steps of then young leaders Fidel Castro, Che Guevara and others during the Cuban Revolution. I asked several questions as we ventured along the hike, much to my student's amusement. Additionally, we were climbing a Cuban mountain in June. The heat was brutal. I had questions about when and where we were stopping.

Afternoon class in the hotel lobby

As we started walking, I noticed there was no path. My American mindset prevailed as I searched for paved and well-manicured paths with warning signs and guard rails. None of these luxuries were present. No pavement, no path, no guardrail, and no signs. I asked more questions like, "Why isn't this path paved if the tours have been ongoing for decades?" We were going through rugged terrain, and most of us did not have appropriate shoes or attire. There was a lot of grunting, high steps, lifting the weight of your entire body to climb the rocks, pushing each other, holding each other up, guiding each other by holding hands, pulling each other out of mud holes, and trusting the path to find the way in the absence of signs. The colorful language amongst us was real. We were all frustrated and not even halfway through the hike.

I quickly realized that my A-type personality students and especially me had to give up our need for control and Americanized expectations to make it through the mountains.

Through falls, scrapes, bruises, broken fingernails, mud holes, dangling tree branches, slippery slopes, emotional breakdowns, and inspiring each other to persevere, we were all pushed beyond our perceived abilities and made it through the mountain of adversity.

Cuba is more than a study trip destination to complement the Global Education course. It is a learning experience filled with understanding the connections within the African Diaspora, learning in transit, self-discovery, and growth, and knowledge of a beautiful country filled with a rich and often misunderstood history, culture, politics, and people. It is the trip of a lifetime and a learning experience accompanied by an open mind and heart.

References

Keeton, M. T., & Tate, P. J. (1978). Learning by Experience—What, Why, I-low. *Jossey-Bass.*

Kolb, D. A. (2014). *Experiential learning: Experience as the source of learning and development.* FT press.

About the Author

Andrea Lewis is Director of Student Success and Associate Professor of Education at Spelman College. Her major research interests include teacher preparation, social class and education, and Black girls in majority schools. Email: alewis29@spelman.edu

Chapter Thirteen

Wuothi Eka Inee!

Travel as a Tool for Self-Discovery and Agent of Transformation

Catherine Odari

Spelman College, USA

"The world is a book and those who do not travel read only a page" is a dictum that has been attributed to St. Augustine, although the real source is contested. Nevertheless, it is true that traveling, much like reading a book, affords one the opportunity to discover both the world and oneself. More importantly, it empowers one to challenge and rethink the societal norms and expectations that shaped their worldview. The experiences and exposure to alternative ways of living that global travel accords one, opens the eyes to new possibilities. That was my experience after I moved to the United States. Prior to my travel, my views and perspectives on social issues had primarily been informed and shaped by my socio-cultural and Christian upbringing in Kenya.

GENDER RELATIONS

Although I had interacted with groups from diverse backgrounds during my matriculation from primary to university, the patriarchal social norms of my Luo ethnic group shaped my interactions and perspectives on gender relations. Traditionally among the Luo community, female gender roles were distinct and situated primarily within the domestic sphere. They were characterized by acts of service to the men, such as cooking and serving them, cleaning after them, doing their laundry, taking care of the children, and even offering/surrendering a seat to them at social gatherings. The latter act of service was especially expected of married women (known as *wagogni*) visiting their maternal homes. This sub-set of Luo women were often forbidden from inheriting property from their parents because it was assumed that they would be married and inherit from their husbands' families. Thus, a Luo woman's existence was steeped in domesticity, so much so that to a large extent, her worth was based on her ability to be married regardless of her other professional achievements. For example, growing up, I would hear unmarried young women being told that they needed to learn how to cook *ugali* (a staple in many Kenyan communities) or risk their husbands sending them back to their maternal homes (a practice associated with stigma). Hence, moving to America to attend graduate school marked the beginning of my questioning some of these "norms."

One such moment occurred when a male professor invited all graduate students in the class to dinner at his house. The professor's female partner was also a faculty member in the same department. So, when we arrived at their home, I expected to find the wife preparing dinner for the guests while he sat comfortably on the couch reading or watching tv as I had been accustomed to seeing gender roles play out in my African setting. Instead, what I encountered baffled me at the time. It was the male professor who was in the kitchen preparing lasagna for dinner, while his partner entertained the guests! When we finished having dinner, he loaded the dishes in the dishwasher and cleaned the pots. More confounding to me at the time was the fact that, not only was he, "the man of the house," doing the domestic chores, but he was also about my father's age and a professor! I had never seen a man of my father's age take on domestic chores as he did. Additionally, by virtue of his status as a professor, in my culture, he would be expected to have a house help. Men of his caliber simply did not step into the kitchen!

My experience at that dinner forced me to rethink my understanding of social norms. I realized that they are not universal and are sometimes socially constructed to serve the interests of certain dominant groups in the society, in this case, Luo men. I began to understand how a practice that I had become accustomed to and thought to be universal could be nefarious and damaging, especially when examined in the context of how overworked and underappreciated some Luo women were. I reasoned that if norms are created, they can also be deconstructed and, if necessary, reconstructed in ways that are less oppressive to the overall community. However, the thought of reconceptualizing my cultural norms was both nerve-wrecking and exciting. I wondered if this would entail relinquishing a part of my culture and embracing a new one, a foreign one, a western one, the implications of which were unnerving – was I becoming "Americanized?" In the end, I concluded that in life we grow, we encounter new ideas, and our thought processes change. Thus, I owe it to my cultural group to challenge ideas that are antithetical to the wellbeing of its members, in this case, the women of the Luo community, even if the consequences are uncomfortable.

IDENTITY

Growing up in Kenya, it never crossed my mind to introduce myself as a Black woman; after all everybody is black with a few exceptions. Majority of the population identified with either the region they came from or their ethnic group. It was not unusual to hear someone ask me what ethnic group I came from, and if they already knew that I was Luo, they would proceed to ask what region or clan I belonged to. Thus, moving to the US thrust me into a world of a new identity that did not only designate who I was, but also came with preconceived notions about Black girls and women. It was a racialized identity that I had not experienced before. It made me rethink how I conceptualize identity because it made me hyper aware of who I am in every space that I entered and defined how I carried myself. Identity to me was no longer just who I am, the lineage or heritage I came from, or the social norms I participated in. I was no longer a woman from the Luo community, but a Black woman in America.

But was being a Black woman enough to describe who I was? Did I have to surrender who I was when I was in Kenya, or being a Black a woman was just adding another layer to my identity? I grappled with these questions and particularly with what would happen to my other identity – the one I had known from birth. So, I began to rethink the ways I would reassert my Africanness, my Kenyaness, and my Luoness. I found myself listening to very old Luo rhumba music that my parents listened to in the 70s and 80s. I would adorn beaded jewelry that was handmade in Kenya. I would try my best not to speak in English with any Kenyan I encountered. I cooked Kenyan food frequently and connected with as many Kenyans as I could on social media, some of whom I had never met. I used these strategies to reassert my identity to myself. They were my ways of restoring my authenticity. Ironically, these were things we took for granted while in Kenya, sometimes preferring to listen to western music, eat western food, and watch western shows and movies.

Later, I realized that this is something that many immigrants go through when they move to a foreign country, especially to the western countries. It suddenly dawns on them that the country they have immigrated to is structured around people's identities, especially racial identity, forcing them to look back to their cultural heritage for a sense of belonging. Ironically, those who never listened to their traditional songs or spoke their languages in favor of western languages like English or French begin to express interest in learning their native language, eating their native food, and listening to their native music. Although I was not one of the extreme cases because I speak my native language, I found myself trying to find opportunities to speak it more. I was content to be both a Black woman and a Luo woman and not just either/or.

CONCLUSION

Overall, these two experiences taught me about the fallibility of every culture. No matter how attached we are to our specific cultural group or nation-state, we should understand that they are flawed and be open to critiquing those aspects that are oppressive and strive to make changes no matter how difficult or uncomfortable they are. After all, the success of the community depends on its humility in accepting its fallibility and willingness to implement changes that serve them better. Otherwise, the community risks losing its legitimacy in the eyes of its members.

About the Author

Catherine Odari, is an assistant professor in the department of History at Spelman College. Her major research interests are Colonialism and Trans-national liberation movements in Eastern Africa, Migration and Diaspora, and the intersections of race, class and gender in the colonial and post-colonial periods. Email: codari@spelman.edu

Chapter Fourteen

Exposure

In honor of Richard and Corrine Ganz

Margery A. Ganz

Spelman College, USA

Exposure was the term that my parents used with my brother and me when we were growing up. I can't remember a time that my parents didn't talk about current events at dinner or watch the news together at 11:00; my father called it "exposure "-- whether it was learning to play an instrument, going to live classical music or live theater, going to an arts camp in Michigan, going to museums, or traveling in the US and overseas. They wanted us to become global citizens long before that term was popular. They believed that a global outlook or perspective developed from the kind of experiences they provided for me and my brother.

My brother, Robert Ganz, spent the summer after his bar mitzvah camping in National Parks across the United States. After he graduated from a Quaker high school in 1969, he spent the summer in Tanzania on a service project building, a farm storage building for a secondary school outside of Dar es Salam. That same summer I had my first solo experience in Italy, which dramatically changed my life. While I had taken a five day trip to Montreal with my family and also attended a s music camp in Michigan, the trip to Italy was my first time using a passport, traveling by myself, and spending 8 weeks in another culture—with a different language, strange food, and seeing the remains of an ancient civilization. I spent the summer of 1967 in Verona, Italy,as part of The School of International Training's (SIT) "World Learning" and "The Experiment in International Living."

Study abroad was not popular or developed at that time and "The Experiment" promised a wonderful experiential program, full of cultural experience-s from camping in the

Dolomites to sightseeing in Venice, Orvieto and Rome as well as afew days at the beach in Livorno. Our group of ten young women, chaperoned by a male Mormon group leader (Spencer Snow) who had been a missionary in Europe, was phenomenal. We learned about Italian culture and food, we taught them (the Italians) our culture as well. I went with my Italian family to church on Sundays, and I took them to synagogue with me one Friday night. My host family did not know there was a synagogue in Verona, and I did not know that Romeo and Juliet were real people and that Juliet lived in a castle in downtown Verona. In fact, I spent my 20th birthday posing on Juliet's balcony at a party given by the city's tourism office. In the Teatro Romana we saw Shakespear's *The Merchant of Venice* and at the L'Arena di Verona we saw two operas.

In return, some of our group members invited our host families for an American cook-out, with hamburgers, hotdogs, and all the trimmings. The butcher around the corner would not sell us as much meat as we wantedwithout first calling our Italian moms, as he thought it was way too much meat for our families. As a special treat for my birthday, I learned to eat rabbit and squid ink risotto. These were true challenges, but I had to eat them as those dishes were part of the the dinner entrees, in my honor.

Living as a member of an Italian family that summer changed my life forever in multiple ways. I fell in love with Italy's language, food, culture, and history. It reaffirmed my plans to become a historian andchanged the focus of my research from England or France in the Middle Ages to Florence in the Renaissance. Seeing all those fabulous works of art and architecture so amazed me that I felt like I had to return and dig more deeply into Florence's history and art of that time period. Though I received no academic credit for my summer in Italy, I became irrevocably committed to life as a scholar/teacher of the Italian Renaissance. I am still the 3rd child of my Italian family and see them frequently when I am in Italy on research trips, and they have visited me in Atlanta. My "Italian niece" has always had Spelman tee shirts. As she says, "Anyone can buy a Harvard tee shirt here in Verona, but it is more special to have a Spelman one." And now they are being worn by her kids,who call me their American aunt. Arelationship from an 8 week summer program has continued for more than 50 years.

My next trip to Italy was longer. I spent a year mostly in Florence,working on my doctoral dissertation in the Archivio di Stato in Florence and the Vatican Library and Secret Archives in Rome. Living ona fifth floor walk-up, some 86 steps up, meant true exercise, but the views were definitely worth the effort: the dome of the Duomo from one window and the Pza. Santa Croce from another. Spending time reading state/public documents, as well as private journals, *ricordanze,* tax statements, wills,and letters, all contributed to the picture of social and political fabric of this period which I could teach about at Spelman. Teaching at a women's college for 40 years has led me to modify my research agenda to include more about Florentine women than ever imagined.

I came to Spelman in August 1981 to teach European history and World Civilization (the precursor of ADW), which was being developed as a two-semester requirement that summer. Due to a fall the first day of school, I was down a course that I did not want to teach anyway. Dr. Donald Stewart, who was president at that time, asked me to help send Spelman women abroad, since I had spent time living overseas and was familiar with the process. I was happy to take on that task and I acquired a new title my first week in Atlanta—I became the Study Abroad Adviser. I didn't realize how my life would change as a result of that request. In the early years, as "Go Away Lady," I spent hours trying to convince students to have an experience outside Spelman's gates. As a result, we went from 2 students abroad in 1982 to where we are now—in a normal year some 400+ students on summer and semester credit-bearing programs overseas. I spent more time during my 40 years at Spelman doing study abroad than teaching history. The leadership provided by Dr. 'Dimeji Togunde, our Vice Provost for Global Education, has greatly increased our numbers and has led us to rank higher than I ever expected Spelman could reach in The Institute of International Education's annual ratings.

From that first trip to Italy in 1967, I have returned to Italy more than 25 times to continue my research, to create a circle of Italian friends, and to create a summer program for Spelman students in Ferrara. Italy is truly my second home. While Italy is still my number one country for living abroad, as Spelman's Director of Study Abroad, I have visited more places in the world than I thought possible. My passports contain stamps from some 55 countries, many of which I never expected to visit, and I hope to add more. My travels have taken me from Atlanta to Morocco, Tunisia, Ghana, Tanzania, South Africa, Jordan, Israel, Turkey, India, South Korea, Japan, China, Australia and New Zealand. South America also included top destinations like Argentina, Chile, Brazil, Peru, Trinidad & Tobago, Mexico, Costa Rica, and the Dominican Republic and Cuba. And then, of course, most of Europe. Those experiences overseas also led to my involvement in the Institute for International Public Policy (IIPP), which prepares minority students for careers in both the public and private arenas, such as the State Department, USAID, Peace Corp, United Nations, CIA, and the NGO community. Dr. Tinaz Pavri and I co-chaired the Sophomore Summer Institute on our campus for 4 years. Grants from the Department of Education, Department of State, IIPP, Mellon and other foundations have enabled Spelman and its faculty to create and run programs in non-traditional places like Ankara, Ghana, China, Bahia, Brazil and exchanges with Tsuda College of Women in Japan and a group of British universities.

I never expected to have a career in Study Abroad; I simply thought that I would happily be an Italian Renaissance historian, teach in a college or university and produce scholarship on the social and political history of Florence in the fifteenth century. Instead, due to my parents' belief in the benefits of exposure, I was prepared when asked to try and duplicate my own experiences for Spelman students. My split personality as an academic—Professor of History and Director of Study Abroad and International Exchange—has been the best career imaginable. I have a great group of colleagues all over the world who are part of my study abroad network and my Renaissance history group. In multiple languages, over great food and in fabulous locations I had never imagined going, and at international conferences I have had a spectacular time. I am certain that eventually Covid-19 will pass and we all can return to sending students to study abroad. In addition to my Spelman students, my IIPP fellows and my nieces and nephews I want to acknowledge and thank my parents for exposing me to the various influences and places that have given me such a fulfilling career.

About the Author

Margery A. Ganz, Ph.D., is a Professor Emerita of History, and the former Director of Study Abroad & International Exchange at Spelman College, E-mail: mganz@spelman.edu

Chapter Fifteen

Global Travel Experience

Sallie C. Burns

Spelman College Sisters Chapel, USA

Sometimes history lies not in archives or libraries but beneath our feet.....The Battle of Adwa - Raymond Jonas. This statement from Raymond Jonas fascinates me (I never heard this before, but it's fascinating me too!). I have been fortunate to plan several trips for Student Affairs Global Experience (S.A.G.E.) through Quality Enhancement Plan (QEP). In pre-pandemic history, Spelman thrived on *"Going Global."* But now, in the middle of the pandemic, I think it will be a long time before Spelman would allow for any international trips.

I am the program coordinator for Sisters Chapel, the most prominent building on campus and the heartbeat of Spelman College. I love my work and especially enjoyed planning global trips for students. Seeing the excitement on their faces, when they are chosen, is "priceless"!

The Division of Student Affairs established the Student Affairs Global Experience (S.A.G.E.) program, years ago, to provide global opportunities to learn about diverse cultures and values of the world and to provide global experiences that enable them to function in a multicultural society. S.A.G.E. programs were designed to provide exposure for students to live and work within an increasingly interdependent world, providing them with the leadership skills necessary to both succeed in a global marketplace and understand themselves as intercultural citizens of a global community.

In 2007, Dean Rev. Lisa D. Rhodes partnered with Student Life and Engagement to arrange global trips every other year. Dr. Beverly Daniel Tatum gave an announcement in hopes of providing each student a chance to travel globally (at least one time) before graduation (Wow, how interesting!). I assisted in planning the first global trip with thirty-five students to Senegal, Africa, but did not attend.

Ghana, West Africa

March 2020, I coordinated the trip to Ghana, West Africa, a Sisters Chapel WISDOM Center Empowering Women for Change Study Tour. I was extremely grateful when Dr. Rhodes asked me to join the trip because of my organizational skills in planning the previous trip. In my preparation for the trip, nothing could prepare me for what I felt when I stepped off the plane in our Motherland. I felt the presence of ancestors, their struggles, their love, and their survival for life! Yes, "sometimes history lies not in archives or libraries but beneath our feet." I felt the earth move because I was walking in the footsteps of our ancestors (that's touching). Many of us began to cry because it felt so good to be "home"! A home I had thought about many times from my African book on my coffee table. There was a cultural and personal value to going *home*, a paradigm shift, you might say. I will never forget the visit to the Cape Coast Castle (in fact, we had the same tour guide, our President Barack Obama and family had a year earlier), a female and young children's dungeon where our ancestors faced the *Door of No Return*. We stood boldly and sang the Spelman Hymn in the dungeon (this feels heavy).

Years ago, a friend traveled to his home in Cape Town, South Africa, and gifted me with a beautiful cloth painting of an African marketplace and a book of Africa. I had the picture framed, and it now resides on my living room wall. The book spoke volumes to the lives of many African marketplaces and "to see pictures come to life" was more than I could imagine. I saw women with babies tied to their backs or fronts and well-balanced baskets atop their heads, as they sold their goods, unfamiliar fruits and vegetables. Never in my wildest dreams did I think I would be planning international trips for students, and be a travel coordinator on all international trips hosted by Sisters Chapel.

Cape Town, South Africa

In Cape Town, South Africa, we partnered with Health Careers. The goal was again to support the QEP to increase learning abilities by comparing cultural differences and similarities based on our engagement and conversations related to political, economic, educational, religious, and gender issues. The students participated in civic engagement and community services within the global community; and experienced cultural engagement that reflected a personal definition and understanding of cultural, religious, and spiritual diversity. Through reading, discussion, journaling, reflection, and meaningful engagement with faculty, students, African women scholars, religious leaders, and political prisoners, Spelman students expanded their understanding of slavery, apartheid, African Traditional Religious Culture, and African women's agency. It was depressing to see the cell in which President Nelson Mandela was held captive for twenty-seven years. Humanitarian acts through community service projects were done, which helped to facilitate a holistic study tour experience. Visits to a medical center, gave the students a glance from a healthcare perspective on economics.

Students Explore Trinidad and Tobago

In 2012, thirty Spelman students, faculty, and staff traveled to Trinidad and Tobago with Health Career as partners again. As another part of the Student Affairs Global Experience (SAGE) program, this short-term study tour was designed to support the Spelman College mission through students' educational experience and cultural engagement. Students broaden their understanding of Caribbean culture through various readings, discussions, reflections, and community service. During the study tour, students also visited with Caribbean women executives, journalists, educators, policy makers, and religious leaders, and engaged in conversation with faculty and students at Trinidad's South-West Regional Health Authority and the University of West Indies, Medical and Nursing Schools. The trip highlighted the intersections between social and political systems, economic factors, and religious life as they seek to support the learning goals of the Quality Enhancement Plan (QEP).

2018 Health Careers Program Global Experience Cape Town, South Africa

Because of my organizational skills in planning international trips and partners in other trips, Dr. Roslyn Gregory Bass asked me to spearhead the Cape Town, South Africa trip with Health Career students. Participants were selected based on their scholastic achievements and their commitment to pursuing a career in the health profession.

South Africa is a phenomenal country and truly has made unique contributions to the field of medicine. Students were exposed to a diverse clinical setting, heard from experts in the field of HIV and Heart Disease, and learned of the triumphant accomplishments of the people in the region. Along with the tours, students were challenged to conduct a research project to enhance their inquiry skills, critical thinking, written and oral communication skills. We worked hard on providing a well-rounded experience for each student. Our academic and exploratory tours included the University of Western Cape, the Red Cross Pediatric Hospital, HIV Research Center, and other Healthcare facilities. Of course, we could not miss visits to the Apartheid Museum, Table Mountain, and Robben Island (prison and leprosy camp).

2018 Students explore Rome and Florence, Italy

Eighteen students and six staff members made their way to beautiful Rome and Florence, Italy, during the winter break. This trip was truly fascinating. Italy was the epicenter of powers for centuries. The students were excited to wander among the ancient grounds and buildings of the Roman Forum, the Colosseum, and St. Peter's Basilica. We found out that the Roman Forum was where elections, public speeches, and gladiator matches were held. Even trials of accused criminals took place on the steps of Forum. The giant stones that built the Roman Forum and Colosseum made you wonder how slaves carried them to build such magnificent structures. We marveled at the exquisite paintings in the Sistine Chapel. The Vatican, the Holy place gave way to the spiritual side of the trip. Students were fascinated to know that the items they brought at the Vatican could be blessed by bishops of the Vatican. There were self-guided tours of Rome and Florence, and the cuisine was superb, mostly pasta and pizza. The wine was a staple at lunch and dinner for Italians; teenagers could begin drinking wine at the tender age of 16 (our students were shocked to learn that teenagers could drink legally so early in life). In Florence, we visited the Leaning Tower of Piazza, a sight truly to be seen by the naked eye. We visited the Duomo and Accademia, while taking in every sight and sound of this 'fabulous' city. We can't forget the shopping, the students were in heaven, because named brand companies originated in Italy, such as Gucci, Louis Vuitton, Versace, Dolce e Gabbana, and many more. We had such a great time shopping, so wonderful that many of us had to purchase extra luggage to transport our wonderful finds back home (that's interesting!). Many students said they brought Christmas presents for their family and friends (that's really sweet).

The international trips poured into me a hunger to visit more countries, learn from and immerse into diverse cultures. "I shall never forget the blessings bestowed upon me to organize international trips", and to be able to travel with students, faculty and staff was an added value. (It's amazing to see your grateful attitude! Beautifully written, with much clarity. I learned quite a bit about Spelman, Africa and Italy. and enjoyed reading it. Congratulations!)

About the Author

Sallie C. Burns was the program coordinator and assistant to the Dean of the Sisters Chapel at Spelman College. She earned a BA degree in Organizational Management from Morris Brown College and an MBA from Shorter College.

Chapter Sixteen

Study Travel as an Extension of a Familiar Place

Rosalind Gregory-Bass

Spelman College/ Costa Rica, South Africa, Trinidad and Tobago

My quest for global travel stems from an inner desire to be infinite. Infinite thinking eliminates the notions of boundaries and limits. It fuels my desire to be connected to the diasporic regions of the world that connect me to others individually and as a collective. As a physician and professor in higher education, I am keenly aware of how my experiences shape my perspectives as an inquiry-based learner and critical thinker. I strongly encourage my students to engage in global exchanges to inform their ideals and practices. seek to be and Merriam-Webster's Dictionary formally describes a diaspora as the movement, migration, or scattering of a people away from an established or ancestral homeland. Even though the term initially was coined to describe the dispersion of Jewish people, the African Diaspora dates back to 1500 A.D. The countries affected the most by the African Diaspora, that today have the highest number of people of African descent, include Brazil, the United States, Haiti, the Dominican Republic, Columbia, France, Venezuela, Jamaica, the United Kingdom and Mexico (https://www.worldatlas.com/articles/where-is-the-african-diaspora.html). Unfortunately, global silos exist, thus blurring the connections between these countries. Traveling and developing meaningful connections with the people and the culture with whom I am connected is a passion and intellectual complement to my origins as a woman of Gullah Heritage. J. Lord Matory highlights in his JSTOR article Gullah heritage is exceptionally "authentic" in their preservation of African culture in the US due to their "isolation." (https://daily.jstor.org/the-cosmopolitan-culture-of-the-gullah-geechees/).

The Gullah Heritage of Sea Islands of South Carolina is entrenched in African beliefs and cultural ties of our diasporic origins. The Gullah people are descendents of enslaved Africans from west and central Africa who reside along the intercoastal waterway of both Georgia and South Carolina. The islands are displayed in figure 1. Our family history is preserved in church records and on gravestones that date back to slavery. My father's descendents were brought to Edisto Island and migrated to Wadmalaw Island and my mother's descendents resided north of the Charleston Peninsula, on Bull's Island and Cainhoy.

There is a deep connection to God, spirituality, family, and the belief that we are connected within the universe. This belief of "one" guides our religious practices, celebrations, community events, and how we treat our neighbor. This belief and way of life allow me to see the interconnectedness of a people torn from their homeland.

I take my heritage with me as I travel to foreign lands, that in so many ways feel very familiar. And even though this is a personal journey, my mission as a research scholar and professor is to impart this experiential knowledge of history, science, politics, and the impact of economic stability to the next generation of global citizens.

Children of the Diaspora

What does it mean to have two homes and feel like a foreigner in both? One home that is familiar and the other that you have yet to fully explore. This is the dilemma of children of the African Diaspora. I was born at a Jewish Hospital in the South Bronx neighborhood surrounded by Black Americans, Puerto Ricans, and people from the Dominican Republic. In the early 60's, my Gullah family (who migrated from the segregated south in the late 50's and early 60's to NY) moved from the south Bronx to Queens. I attended an all-Black and Puerto Rican Catholic School to embark on a middle-class US experience. We engaged with grocers and butchers from Italy and Chinese vendors who laundered clothing. Having my formative years in New York gave me a global experience within the borders of the United States. These local experiences were also coupled with international experiences at a young age.

I recall having an intergenerational travel experience abroad to multiple Caribbean islands with my grandfather, a former US Coast Guard, which ignited my family's interest in geographic discovery. Since that time, I have traveled back to the Bahamas four times. I have also traveled to Jamaica, St. Martin, St. Maarten, the Cayman Islands, Trinidad and Tobago, and the Dominican Republic. Having these Caribbean experiences first provided context and familiarity with my friends and associates I spent time with in New York City. Years later, my Mexican and Central American experiences included Cozumel, Cancun, and Costa Rica, respectively. My European travel is limited to the United Kingdom (London), France (Paris), and Spain (Barcelona). Domestically, I have traveled to multiple states and Canada (Vancouver, Toronto, Montreal, and Quebec). But the most impactful and emotional experience to date was my trip to Cape Town, South Africa. Even though I did not deplane in Ghana and Senegal, the view from my airplane window was enough to reconnect me with the spirit of my ancestors, who paid the ultimate sacrifice for my existence and voluntary return to a place that feels like "home." This reconnection is not a fleeting, intangible feeling. It was definitely palpable. For me, it is a rush of emotions that makes me question, "what if?" What if western and central Africa were not colonized, exploited, and its people violently sold? What if they did not survive the middle passage? What if they did not survive the brutality of captures and plantation owners? What if I had an opportunity to live in a country where my existence as a human is not questioned and value was not monetized? The ultimate sacrifice to survive and to maintain language, foods, music, spirituality, and medicinal practices is what became immediately present in the forefront of my mind. Since Gullah culture helped me to maintain so many of those aspects of west African culture, I did not feel like a stranger in a foreign land.

My formal training at Spelman College in the biomedical sciences gave me a wider lens to view the world. Spelman College, a historically Black college, helped me to not only appreciate the cultural similarities and differences in food, music, art, politics, and religious practices, but it gave me an opportunity to look at the health and wellness of a nation. Spelman provided this avenue for critical analysis and I am beyond grateful.

COSTA RICA

My first adventure was to Costa Rica. The goal was to evaluate the Environmental Science program in Monteverde and Tropical Studies Program at LaSelva Field Station. Landing in San Jose, C.R. was associated with feelings of uncertainty, given my limited Spanish fluency and the fact that I was traveling solo. However, upon landing in this beautiful country, I was immediately greeted with the "Pura Vida" (Pure Life) culture and the warmth of a people whose melanin spectrum mimicked that of the United States.

Traveling to the cloud forest in Monteverde with my colleagues from other US colleges and universities was an adventure, but worth the ride. I was immediately struck by the flora and the massive tree canopy. It was in Monteverde that I truly gained an even deeper appreciation for biology and knew that these excursions could no longer be solo, but that students had to be with me. A slide presentation could in no way do it justice. This is also where I began to hear about the world-renowned medical system in Costa Rica and how they excelled at universal healthcare, ensuring that all of their citizens, regardless of socioeconomic status, would receive excellent treatment. I also tapped into my Gullah heritage that focused on use of land and its flora to provide medicinal healing in times of need. Costa Ricans, old and young, were familiar with the scientific names of plants, roots, and other natural substances and the impact they had on human systems. When asked how they were so knowledgeable about botany, they described their universal commitment to sustainability. which requires citizens to be knowledgeable about their environment. The respect for nature made Costa Rica feel like home.

CAPE TOWN, SOUTH AFRICA

Cape Town was also a once in a lifetime experience. The Spelman College Student Affairs Global Experience (SAGE) program to the continent of Africa with the Dean of the Chapel was an exciting trip to consider. The SAGE program takes new proposals each year and this was the first of its kind to combine medicine and religion. The Health Careers Program was invited to include an emphasis on healthcare in the region. From the pre-trip orientations to the nightly debriefing after each excursion, I was again experiencing an awakening that bridged my Gullah American heritage and religious practices with South African culture. The demographic characterization of people and tribal groups reminded me of the melting pot of New York. I also could appreciate both its metropolitan and rural landscapes. As I sat atop Table Mountain, one of few wonders of the world, I was speechless by the beauty and majestic nature of this national landmark. Another speechless moment was when we visited the Langa Township to learn of the segregated practices of the Dutch during Apartheid. This was not just a story of segregation and oppression, but a testimony about resilience and social justice. I learned of how doctors, teachers, and lawyers remained in the townships to embrace their heritage and to stay connected to their people, their traditions, and places of worship. There was still an admiration for not just Mandiba (Nelson Mandela), as he is affectionately called in South Africa, but for all members of the resistance who dared not to be defined by their circumstance. All these sociopolitical conversations were present as the group discussed the health and wellness of the nation during our evening reflections. The reflections gave students and opportunity to unpack similarities and differences seen between the US and Cape Town. Faculty facilitated these discussions using prompts and also relying on student comments to guide the conversation.

At the Sarah Barton Residential Center for Domestic Violence, the students and faculty saw how the impact of protests and resistance turned inward to affect the most vulnerable. It was explained that energy, anger, frustration, and violent acts toward the Afrikaners was transferred to women and children after apartheid ended. One theory is explained by Sideris and Benjamin, where they highlight, " South Africa's transition from apartheid to political democracy has been marked by a sudden and intense disruption of norms and identities. Challenges to previously held values have made their way into the personal and private domains of people's lives, to make practices in intimate relationships sites of contestation. The issue of sexual violence has occupied a central place in exposing the realms of intimacy to public scrutiny. In the aftermath of the transition to democracy sexual violence became an unprecedented focus of public concern and debate, with relational and sexual practices, in particular those of men, increasingly interrogated." (https://www.jstor.org/stable/10.18772/2013046031?turn_away=true)

Directly related but not mutually exclusive to the increase in violence is the backdrop of the Human Immunodeficiency Virus (HIV) Pandemic. We spoke candidly with University of Western Cape representatives and clinicians at the Red Cross Children's Hospital. The only other children's facility is in Egypt. This is significant given the high incidence and prevalence of babies born with HIV during the height of the pandemic.

They discussed how HIV impacted the social, political, and economic infrastructure of the country. The hospital is the only pediatric hospital south of the equator. We learned of the stigmatization of having a positive status and the myths around the prevention, diagnosis, and treatment of the infection. Unfortunately, these myths keep citizens from using best practices to eradicate the rising incidence and prevalence of disease.

This trip was also focused on retracing the steps of Nelson Mandela at Robbin Island. To understand Nelson Mandela's desire to live is still baffling after seeing the condition by which he and other inmates were forced to endure. Whether the mental health challenges from years of confinement or the physical challenges of hard labor in the limestone quarry, it again defines the resilience of a people who sacrifice for the greater good. The spirit of ONE. Again, I felt like I was home.

TRINIDAD AND TOBAGO

For their next trip, this same team of Health Careers Program and Sisters Chapel staff decided to embark on a trip to Trinidad and Tobago. We focused on high priority items, such as didactic seminars by the University of West Indies Faculty, reflection seminars by Spelman College Faculty, and interdisciplinary healthcare experiences. Those experiences included the politics of healthcare (Ministry of Health), social justice and advocacy (with not-for-profit agency-Ms. BraFit), economics (public vs private healthcare facilities), and the social science of race, gender, class (individual interviews with numerous citizens).

Other cultural aspects of the trip were addressed in traveling to different regions of the country with non-healthcare related experiences (i.e., tour of Tobago, local church services, visits to both inner-city and suburban areas of the country). As an all-women's college, working with the Association of Female Executives of Trinidad and Tobago (AFETT) was important when addressing the mission and strategic plan of our institution. Speaking with an alumna continued to provide the students with an authentic perspective of life as a physician on the island.

Experiential learning is an equal collaboration with all entities to ensure a well-rounded interdisciplinary education for both faculty and students. Faculty learn about pedagogical and programmatic similarities and differences among institutions. Likewise, students can gain valuable information that enriches their overall academic and career development. Personally, I gained valuable insight into the food and dialect of Trinidadians that reminded me of the cuisine and language of Gullah/Geechee people on the sea islands of South Carolina. This experience was even more meaningful, since my daughter, a sophomore at Spelman, had an opportunity to travel with us. To have this unique time together as mother and daughter (while also being faculty and student) was indescribable. Again, I experienced home on another island of the African Diaspora.

The culmination of these experiences profoundly impacted how I designed the new Health Science major at Spelman College. One core foundational component of the curriculum focuses on a student learning outcome (SLO), which seeks to assess students on their knowledge of the African Diaspora and its impact on healthcare. Three courses were designed to support this SLO: Introduction to Health Science, Race, Gender and Medicine: 21st Century Health Disparities, and 21st Century Global Health. The latter comes as a result of two study travel experiences that focus on global health. The outcomes of this experience have been impressive and significant. We can confidently report that of our first two cohorts of Health Science majors, 95% have had a study travel experience.

IMPACT

Overall, my personal connection to the Diaspora has led me to provide similar experiences for diverse students and added to the interdisciplinary perspectives of the nation's future healthcare workforce. I am beyond thankful for these opportunities, and I'm hopeful that they have connected students to places that may feel like a familiar place, like home.

About the Author

Rosalind Gregory-Bass is an Associate Professor in the Environmental and Health Science Department and Director of the Health Careers Program. Her major research interests lie in the area of women's health, global health, cancer biology, and the elimination of health disparities. Email: rbass@spelman.edu

Chapter Seventeen

Japan

Tales of an Alternate Reality

Chanelle Cunningham

Spelman College, USA

I have many pictures and videos from my time in Japan, but I often think about the moments that I did not have captured on my camera roll. That's where my sense of gratitude kicks in because at least there are numerous experiences that I *do* have record of. But the real "a-ha" moment was the realization that the most impactful memories that I have from Japan are experiences that were never captured on camera. To be honest, the most touching and funny encounters were seen through my *eyes* and not my camera lens. I believe it's like that for most events in life.

In addition to studying in the country, I also had the opportunity to spend time helping at some local after school programs in my free time. Being part of a small moment in a child's life whom you will never see again is powerful. You get to be a part of their life story, as they become a part of yours. I didn't know what the students were saying because I didn't speak Japanese, but I felt their energy. Luckily body language, mannerisms, and expressions are universal languages. Because of that, I'll never forget how laid-back 8th grade Keita was, how bubbly 4th grade Misa was, how meek 10th grade Sawa was. Snapshot memories like those have the ability to make one reflect on other fleeting moments. Everybody you pass on the train or on the street has a story. Before moving to Japan, I had never been exposed to so many people–which ultimately sparked an epiphany-like connection. I'm from a suburban town in Kentucky, where I never took public transportation because my area wasn't set up for it. My first time riding a bus, train, subway or even using a crosswalk was in Nagoya, Japan. That experience was a culture shock, especially being a Black foreigner in a homogenous nation. Even in my current home base of Georgia, my family and I continue to travel everywhere by car as we're still not close enough to the city to necessitate public transport.

Living in Japan was a paradigm shift as I had never noticed just how secluded I was from the world. Although I'm glad not to have to use the western transport system due to my geographical proximity and the privilege of owning a vehicle, the revelation still holds true. I still went from the suburbs of Kentucky to the suburbs of Georgia without much interaction with the people outside my small network, which consists of people I know from work, occasional church and sporadic social functions. Even my college life was not residential. Everything was so contained, so predictable, so habitual, not at all like the spontaneity of passing thousands of people a day on the streets of Tokyo. Crossing paths with a person for one moment to ask for directions, then parting ways and likely never seeing them again.

Living abroad changed my perspective on life and awakened a sense of mindfulness I didn't know existed. Japan broke the monotony in my life and helped me branch out and see there's more to life than going to school, going to work and going home, (with a movie date sprinkled in here and there). I got to be a floating helper in several schools in Japan, so my work was anything but mundane. The different schools required varying modes of transportation, so I never saw the same person every day. The country's low crime rate and safe nature allowed me the freedom to veer off into unknown territory without fear of personal safety. A rare treat that I never had in my home country. So, there were days when I would walk to the train station and then spontaneously decide to turn down a different path just to see where it would take me, and one day, it led me to a park full of cherry blossom trees that rained pink leaves when the wind blew.

On the days that I wasn't volunteering or taking classes, the unscheduled time presented even more of a shift in my schedule because I got to see different parts of Japan that weren't advertised in the media. Personal excursions showed me different landscapes and architecture. I saw apartment buildings the same size as large corporations and was enamored. The novelty behind this opportunity was having exposure to the "hidden" parts of Japan that aren't promoted on TV or in travel magazines. The quaint countryside of Inazawa, the forgotten roads of Tajimi, the working-class town of Hongo, to name a few. I once ended up in a town that was so rural my Google maps couldn't even direct me out. Nobody was outside so I flagged down the only car in sight, luckily the driver was a woman who appeared to be my age. I showed her a picture of the train station I needed to find and she actually drove me there! As a personal rule, I do not recommend hitchhiking in any country on this planet, but I felt safe doing it once. I'm good at reading people and without words, I intuitively recognized a kindred spirit. Just as with the non-English speaking children I encountered, this was another example of having more than one way to communicate intention besides spoken word. So, when this kind stranger hopped out of her car and opened the passenger door for me, I felt led to accept her gesture. We talked about nothing because she didn't speak English, but the silence wasn't awkward as it was filled with friendly energy. I got out and bowed to her and she did the same with a huge grin. She didn't drive off until she watched me go inside the station. I'm not sure if that's the positivity of Japan as a country or the positivity I attract because of the kind of person I am. Either narrative is fine with me.

There were many times when I wanted to go home to the United States because I missed my family, certain foods and hearing the English language on a consistent basis. In light of the pandemic, I now miss living abroad and eating *their* food and hearing *their* language. The saying is true that you don't truly miss something until it's gone. The abrupt closure of borders due to the pandemic helped me realize just how important travel is, especially on an international level. If I had any advice for someone who is considering a global experience, I would say do it. Break out of your comfort zone, cross the imaginary line in the sand your mind creates, get out of the box known as "daily routine". Traveling is a valuable gift that one should cherish because, as evidenced by the pandemic, it could be revoked at any moment. I'm blessed to have experienced pre-COVID travel, but there's no reason that post-COVID travel can't be just as fulfilling. Go wherever that steel bird can take you. Appreciate what you know, embrace what you don't. Redefine the meaning of home and reevaluate the rules you set for your life. All along, there was a version of myself living a self-sufficient, beautiful existence abroad. Had I not made the choice to travel, I wouldn't have met her. Don't be afraid to find yourself.

About the Author

Chanelle Cunningham is a graduate of Spelman College. She obtained her degree in Early Childhood Education and is now an accomplished author, educator and coach who seeks to help others realize that they have the power to write any life story that they choose for themselves. She has lived, worked and studied in Europe, South America and Asia, but currently resides in Georgia. Email: ccunnin6@scmail.spelman.edu

Chapter Eighteen

My Experience as an International Student in the United States

Delvonae Beckles

Spelman College, USA

As a young student growing up in The Bahamas, I would always hear older Bahamians say, "If you want a better education, you should go abroad for college." Of course, we had our own university, but no one seemed to promote it and encourage young Bahamian students to attend. Going "off to school" was always the better choice, if you wanted to be more successful and have a greater quality of life. Obviously, being young and impressionable, and knowing the career I wanted, I decided that I was going to the United States (U.S.) for college. I made this decision early on in my school career and I was probably in the 6th or 7th grade. Like I mentioned earlier, my career choice also played a role in my decision of going to the U.S. for my tertiary education. I wanted to become a pediatrician and I did not know of anyone who was able to become a doctor while staying local. So, what was my exact reason for choosing to go abroad for college as opposed to staying in The Bahamas? I wanted to have an opportunity to attend the best medical schools, and I wanted to have more job opportunities.

THE TRANSITION

It was a huge transition, moving from The Bahamas to the U.S. I was only 16 years old. I was leaving everything behind, specifically my home, my family, and my friends, it was not easy. But let's backtrack to what I had to do before I even started college.

As an International Student, studying in the U.S., I was required to have a student visa. I already had a visitor's visa, but that served me no purpose in this case. The student visa was basically my ticket to a U.S. college, and it gave me permission to study in the States. The process to get a student visa was long and arduous. I had to fill out an application and make an appointment with the U.S. Embassy. Once my appointment date was set, I had to travel to the island of New Providence and complete an interview with the embassy workers. I was asked a series of questions like what my what would my major be and how did I intend to pay for school. I had to have all I's dotted and all T's crossed. In the end, I got approved for my visa and was all cleared to move to the U.S.

So fast forward to move in day, August 2018. It was a great day! My parents were helping me move into college; this was something I was looking forward to for a few months at this point. I did not realize that once my parents left, reality would begin. Leaving home was not easy and when my parents left after moving me in, it felt like the only connection I had left to The Bahamas was gone. For the first two weeks, I had an extreme case of homesickness. I felt like I was in a place where I didn't belong. I was in a new country with no real friends yet, and although I had my college community, I was alone. Yes, everyone else had to leave their family and friends, but no one else understood what it was like to be in a completely different country for the next 4 years. For example, when my American friends could go home for the weekend or for any small break, I could not. They had the resources to see their family whenever they wanted. I was not that fortunate and knew that I would not see my family until the winter and summer breaks. Honestly, it was not feasible to travel such a long distance back to The Bahamas for 3-4 days. So, I had to be content and satisfied with video calls, which was not the same as in person, but it got the job done.

THE DIFFERENCES

Culturally, there were so many differences between the U.S. and The Bahamas. Two of the main differences I noticed were the food and the mannerisms. First, let's talk about the food. Being from the islands, we have our own native dishes that you just can't get anywhere else. An example of what we eat in The Bahamas is peas and rice, fried Snapper, baked macaroni, cracked conch, lobster, coconut tart, and so many more. There was none of that here in America. There were a few foods that I was familiar with, but they just were not prepared the same way I was used to. It took a while for me to adjust to the normal foods eaten by Americans.

Second, the mannerisms of Americans were something I noticed right away. Island people are friendly people. We always smile and say hello to people, even if we do not know them. So, of course, I brought that trait with me to college. I would smile and be courteous to students on campus and was so confused when they would not return the favor. I thought, "Wow, Americans are so mean." It was later on that I came to the realization that different regions in America have different mannerisms. Smiling and speaking to people in passing was more of a southern thing and people from the north did not do that. Learning that, I realized that I could not generalize the entire country and that I should not get offended when someone did not return my friendly gesture.

ADJUSTING TO LIFE IN THE U.S

How did I adjust to life in the United States? Meeting new friends allowed me to become accustomed to living in the U.S. Because most of my friends were Americans, I was able to learn a lot from them about the culture, the history, the norms. Overall, being around them made me feel more comfortable and it gave me a sense of peace and comfort.

I also just let time run its course. I got used to being in the States and living here became normal for me. I still get homesick from time to time but it is nowhere near as bad as it was when I was a freshman. Also, overtime I got familiar with my environment, and I was able to explore more, making the city of Atlanta feel like a second home.

My plan is to remain in America for medical school and potentially start my career here. Since I have been living here on my own, I have developed some independence. As a college student I had to learn how to fend for myself. Yes, I had my parents, but they obviously could not do everything for me. So, this experience has helped me to grow up and become more mature. It has also proven that I am able to face adversities and that I can overcome no matter the circumstance. Do I think that moving to the U.S. for school was a good investment? As a matter of fact, I do. The Bahamas will always be my home and I am not abandoning it. I just decided to choose a path where I could secure a better life for my family and me. Home will always be home and no matter where I choose to go in the world, I will always be a Bahamian.

About the Author,

Delvonae Beckles is a senior, biology major at Spelman College. She is from the beautiful islands of The Bahamas. Delvonae's career goal is to become a pediatrician and then return to The Bahamas to open her own Pediatric Care Center. Email: dbeckles@spelman.edu

Chapter Nineteen

Was It Worth Flying 29 Hours and 25 Minutes?

Diane Ingabire

Spelman College, USA

"Dear Ms. Ingabire: Congratulations! It is an honor to welcome you to the 136th class of Spelman College.". I received the letter in my portal on January 17, 2017. I applied to Spelman without knowing much about the school, but because I was a SHE-CAN Scholar, someone said Spelman would be a good fit for me. Spelman College proved that. I knew it was the right choice for me from the moment I stepped foot on campus.

Let me take you back to when I was preparing to fly to the "land of opportunities," as most people say back home in Rwanda. How does it feel to prepare to leave your family, friends, and the only place you called home. On July 29, 2017, I left my home to move to a new country and continent for four years. Inside me, I was scared and excited at the same time. I was scared because I was leaving my family and friends behind. I did not know what clothes to buy and wondered if they would be fashionable where I was going. I was excited because I did not know what to expect when I landed at the US airport. I left Kigali, Rwanda, on Ethiopian Airlines, with a destination of San Francisco. After 29 hours and 25 minutes of flying over the Mediterranean Sea and the Atlantic Ocean, I made it to San Francisco. Being used to Rwandan time, when I landed in San Francisco, I was 9 hours behind; I was jetlagged. I fought to stay up with others and forced myself to wake up when everyone woke up.

A week after, my body gave up on me. I was super tired, and the energy to see new things disappeared. People back home would ask me to send them pictures of things I see around. They would ask, "Ibiryo byabo bimeze nkibyo mu Rwanda?" (This means is their food like our food?). Because they were eager to know more, I challenged myself to go outside and check things out again. The time came when I had to fly to Atlanta, Georgia, my next home, for four years. I was blessed to have mentors that welcomed me in their families, and they were willing to help me with everything. I flew with them to settle in my new home at Spelman College. Forever grateful to them because every person in a new country appreciates any guidance since everything is new. If I were not with them, I would not have known the best stores to go to and buy room supplies. I would not have known the best winter coats to buy. I would not have purchased rain boots since back home, boots are worn when people are gardening or cultivating. The experience of seeing how little I knew taught me two things; always ask and always be ready to help.

Let's go back to my move-in day at Spelman College. International students moved in a day before others; it was calm; I toured the campus and met the president of Spelman College in Upper Manley (Albert E. Manley College Center). She stopped to say hi to me as a new student, and I felt welcomed to my new home. The next day my roommate moved in; she knew some of the people in Howard-Harreld Hall (HH), and those are the people I hung out with during the week of orientation. Orientation was a tiring week for me, but I learned a lot about Spelman College, given that I knew a few things about the school. Orientation was also fun; a couple of fun activities included learning our dorm's chants and people representing their origins through different songs, which I thought was interesting. I liked how they played music from different US coasts; the then-freshman students would go on stage to represent where they were from in the US. The time reached for international students, and I was sitting in the back of Sisters Chapel, and another international student came and grabbed my hand to dance on stage. I was scared, but I enjoyed the music and danced to it; I remember my roommate joining me on stage. The energy everyone had was unmatched; everyone was friendly. Wow! Again, that moment I knew Spelman was the right place for me.

Throughout the first weeks of school, I struggled with speaking English the whole day. I would call friends from home to talk in Kinyarwanda (my mother tongue) or meet with other Rwandans in the Atlanta University Center (AUC). Of course, that was not the only struggle; academically, I was doing well even though my class participation was at its lowest because I was afraid no one would understand me because of my accent. I struggled to know how to order food at Subway because I did not know the food's name, being asked why I order the same foods every day, and my answer would be "that is what I like." Deep down, it was because I was still learning other foods. I struggled with the variety of drink sizes offered by Starbucks(Tall, Grande, Venti) because I was simply used to small, medium, and large. Also, I spent a long time trying to learn different US coins; at some point, I gave up and decided I would never pay cash to avoid being asked to pay coins or being given coins back. I struggled a lot, but every struggle comes with a lesson. Throughout those times, though, I was making friends. Spelman and Morehouse have a brother-sister exchange tradition for the first-year class, where; I was given a Morehouse brother who became my first close friend. A couple of weeks into school, to tell you how small the world is, a friend of mine from high school (in Rwanda) introduced me to her American friend who was attending Morehouse, and both my Morehouse brother and he became my closest friends on campus. I made friends from different classes, organizations, community services, and they became people with whom I shared different experiences. Together we traveled, danced to Afro-beats, tried new dishes, and celebrated each other's birthdays. The friendships I built are incredible.

My experience at Spelman was mainly great, but sometimes I forced myself to learn things to fit in the community. This included listening to American Rap music often so that I would know some lyrics next time. Are you wondering why that was the case? At most parties, on-campus students would be singing the songs rather than dancing, so I would find myself standing and looking at others singing most of the time. There are things that people do to fit in, so I did that. However, it never changed the fact that I think people should dance if it is a party, so I would always look forward to any party where people are dancing. After my statement above, you might think I hate singing; I do not. I like learning song lyrics, and I realized that people at school sang in some parties' au lieu de dancer (instead of dancing). Most of the songs were not danceable, and singing them would create an entertaining environment.

I was not the only one trying to fit in the Spelman environment. I bet every new student was trying to fit in. Many of us came from different parts of the world, from other states in America, and first-time leaving home. My friends and professors were also trying to learn more about my country and Africa, and I appreciate them having the courage to ask me questions. Some friends wanted to know Kinyarwanda too. I told them I could not teach them to be fluent, but I could teach them a few things like; Bite, umeze ute (Hi, how are you?). I shared Rwandan culture focusing on music, dance, and musical instruments in my Intro to World Music class. I was given a chance to invite my Rwandan friend through zoom, who dances traditional Rwandan dance, to help me through the discussion. You might think I did it because I was part of the class, but my professor invited me again to present in another semester. To this day, I am glad that no one asked me questions like; I have a friend from Nigeria, do you know them? Or do you speak African? I was always open to sharing what I knew about my continent and specifically my country, but if anyone had approached me with those questions, I probably would not have answered them. I liked how most people at Spelman and the AUC were eager to learn, and they would do their research too.

SHE-CAN led me to Spelman, so where did Spelman lead me? I secured internships outside Spelman gates because of the great professors and extraordinary Spelman administrations that ensured students had opportunities through organizing career and school fairs. I received different awards, presented my research at various conferences, and am now pursuing graduate studies. It was worth flying 29 hours and 25 minutes.

About the Author,

Diane Ingabire is a first-year graduate student at Virginia Commonwealth University in the Biomedical Sciences Doctoral Program pursuing a Ph.D. in Pharmacology and Toxicology. Email: ingabirediane72@gmail.com

Chapter Twenty

Brown Girl Meets World

Reflections on Study Abroad

Gretchen Cook-Anderson

Spelman College, USA

In 1888, student Nora Gordon became a pioneer at Spelman College, my alma mater, by studying abroad in the Congo. Exactly a century later in 1988, I followed in her footsteps as a Spelman undergrad on my own journey beyond our American borders for a junior year abroad in Nagoya, Japan. That year, my identity as a Black woman intersected in expected and unexpected ways with my experience.

Most unexpectedly, that was the year that my understanding of the concept of family shifted under feet that walked in far-flung rice fields, on smooth tatami mats, and along chiseled city pavement.

I am the oldest of three siblings born to parents who graduated from Spelman and Morehouse and had lived most of their lives in their Atlanta hometown. The generations before them had also lived and died primarily within a narrow radius of their birth. My parents stretched beyond those boundaries eventually, moving us to the Jersey Shore, then Pittsburgh, and then Columbia, Maryland, where my worldview still consisted mostly of people across the human plane of Black and White and family who all looked like variations of myself.

Studying away in Japan for a full academic year as a Spelman student pushed the seemingly distant, blurry world into vivid color and texture. I didn't know at first what to make of four host sisters – Yoko, Chieko, Kazumi, and Mayumi – and a host mother and father, who spoke only a few words of English. They gestured in ways I did not always grasp, practiced daily customs that required me to quickly shed many of my American habits and expectations, and spoke a dialect of Japanese that sounded even more foreign to my ears than standard Japanese.

I wondered in those first few weeks if I would ever grow comfortable with a culture and family so far removed in distance and custom from my own, or with other American students in my cohort attending Nanzan University who all hailed from vastly different backgrounds.

But, as Japanese scholar and author Okakura Kakuzo said, "The art of life is a constant readjustment to our surroundings." His point of view proved increasingly meaningful to me as I realized how best to acclimate. A few awkward weeks into my life in the Takagi's home, the youngest sister, a 7-year-old, tired of watching me struggle to speak in Japanese, approached me laughing, put her hand up and shouted, "Jan Ken Pon!" I soon realized this was her attempt to play the old-school *"Paper Scissors Rock"* game. Her hand movements made the game clear to me, and we soon launched off into several rounds in both languages. A simple children's game created an instant connection between us. In the months that followed, Kazumi held my hand wherever we went, came to my rescue when she sensed I was experiencing intercultural distress, and hugged me before bed each night.

Her sisters and I too found our own unique ways to connect that transcended language, cultural differences, and race. They began to feel like...family. My Japanese host sisters introduced me to pop culture, food, and nuances of their culture. They gently corrected my mistakes, laughed with me as I adapted to their rituals, and applauded in the moments when I got things right. They were my bellwether of progress in making sense of Japan and both her ancient and contemporary ways.

Adapting to life in Japan also meant figuring out where I fit not only with my Japanese host family but also among other international students. We were all haphazardly tossed together into the program – and like young people often do, thrived despite our differences. My closest band of friends was a motley stew of humanity that most would never have expected.

My Black Girl Magic-self (which I felt as a Spelman woman long before the phrase ever existed!) bonded with a White guy from a small Kentucky town in Appalachia named Brian a Vietnamese-American immigrant named Tuan, a motorcycle-riding Norwegian named Petri, a sunny-spirited Hawaiian of Chinese heritage named Chrissy, a Black student from Amherst College named Eric (we did not expect one another and were each delighted not to be the only Black student on our IES Abroad program), and a freckled, red-headed woman who hailed from Idaho who went by her nickname Kat. We were all together for an entire school year, so I guess it was good we decided early on to make the best of our adventures and our challenges – together.

With them I ate sushi in back-alley restaurants, climbed Mt. Fuji, bathed in hot springs, walked through swampy rice fields, adorned ourselves in kimono and haka on special occasions, enjoyed sumo matches, learned Japanese tea ceremony, did Ikebana flower arranging, sped across Japan on the shinkansen (bullet train), laughed at Japanese comedians on TV, ran through parks filled with the fragrance and beauty of cherry blossoms, and created a strong support network that felt like family, a network spanning time and circumstance that continues more than 30 years later. We also helped each other up when, in the spring of 1989, our Norwegian friend and brother shockingly died in a motorcycle crash just as Japanese azaleas were emerging from winter slumber.

From my familiar, beloved place at Spelman College more than 33 years ago, I launched into travels to 26 countries, where I have widened my global family to include loved ones across Japan, as well as in London, Paris, Brisbane, Cape Town, Amsterdam, Accra, Kigali, Rome, Berlin, Seoul, Barcelona, Granada, Quito, São Paulo, Vienna, Mumbai, Pune, and other cities large and small. This Brown girl knows she's not alone in this world. Along with the 10,000 ancestors who travel with me everywhere I go, these amazing human beings are with me in a shared uplift and lifelong connection that began in many ways with my young host sister reaching out to me through a universal children's game that broke the ice.

In the years since, I have maintained close ties with my Japanese sisters, flying to assist the oldest as she adjusted to being a first-time mom and returning to Japan to both enjoy a reunion with my host family and to sit with my dying host grandfather at his bedside. The pandemic has kept me from visiting the Takagi's, but social media has kept us close.

The experience of scrabbling family together from around the globe has been so profound, as well as ongoing, that it eventually led to more than a decade of my career at IES Abroad dedicated to inspiring nearly 20,000 young people of diverse identities to meet the world beyond our borders – to explore it and find family among strangers. These students have reminded me of myself, this Brown girl in the world, whose life and sense of family was forever transformed at 19 by stepping out on faith and into an international experience.

Chapter Twenty-One

Wanderlust

A Discourse on Living and Learning

Courtney C. Cox

Spelman College, USA

Perhaps travel cannot prevent bigotry, but by demonstrating that all peoples cry, laugh, eat, worry, and die, it can introduce the idea that if we try and understand each other, we may even become friends. ~ Dr. Maya Angelou

The Birth of Wanderlust

My lower and upper school journeys as an International Baccalaureate student ignited my passion for service and traveling the world. I especially loved France and its culture – considering myself a Francophile. Hence, my college double major of International Studies and French. However, as a study-abroad student at Spelman, I had the opportunity to become more fully immersed and engaged in the countries and cultures in which I lived.

As a Rising Sophomore

Inspired and encouraged by my mentor, Professor Norgaisse, my first collegiate international trip was to Fort de France, Martinique at the end of my second semester. There, I reveled in a Francophone Black perspective at the l'université des antilles et la Guyane where I studied French, literature, and history. It was a life-changing experience and my entry into the Négritude movement. I fell in love with the philosophies and writings of Aimé Césaire and Léopold Sédar Senghor. Coupled with ADW, this newly discovered knowledge has forever informed and expanded my worldview and my place in the world as a global citizen.

As a Junior

In Rabat, Morocco, I experienced my "a ha" moment for wanting to pursue law as a profession. My sojourn at L'Ecole Supérieure de Direction et de Gestion in Morocco's capital city exposed me to a country where religion shapes the culture and where the role of women is often unjust and misunderstood. Nonetheless, I sought to immerse myself in the culture; I refused to be an extended-stay tourist. I sought an authentic understanding of the plight of women in Morocco, which led me to volunteer at a women's argan oil cooperative.

My participation involved performing any task needed but most often assisting in the tedious argan extraction process to make argan oil. I also assisted in brainstorming new marketing ideas to advocate the mission of the cooperative. My involvement with the cooperative was the most enlightening aspect of my experience. Conversations with Moroccan women, particularly a woman named Zineb, who revealed her woes as a victim of domestic abuse and her farce of a divorce in a corrupt judicial system, prompted my interest to examine for my thesis the reforms of the Moroccan Family Law Code (Moudawana) enacted in 2004. The reforms exemplified the socio-political and religious dynamics at play in the country, and examination of their successes and limitations further demonstrated Morocco's complexities.

My exposure to injustice, inequality and the study of political ploys and veneers has propelled my desire to advocate change for women globally.

As a Confident Spelman Graduate

As a result of the positive and enriching experiences I had as a study-abroad student, I felt poised and confident enough to fulfill my desire to live in France – at least for a while. My previous travels had equipped me with the skills to adapt to change while living in another culture. So, in the fall of 2012, I lived in Châlons-en-Champange, France for a year working as an English Language Teaching Assistant at Lycée Jean Talon, which is considered a second-rate school. My main duties were to prepare lessons on social issues, political issues, and American culture with emphasis on improving students' English oral expression as well as prepare students for the English portion of the Baccalauréat exam. I used this as an opportunity to enlighten my students about the negative perceptions they had about Black Americans.

Though my primary mission was focused on ameliorating the oral expression of my students in English, my secondary mission was to inspire them to conquer their academic dreams and personal aspirations, to restore their dignity, and to eliminate their sentiments of inferiority as students in a second-class school. To that end, it was my greatest joy to accompany my students on a trip to Kent, England. For many students, this study trip was their first visit to an English-speaking country. They attended classes at the Kent School of English and toured various cities, including the renowned Canterbury. It was gratifying to be able to alleviate many of their fears and anxieties because of my own study abroad experience.

I found that I was simultaneously learning from my colleagues and from my students. On a daily basis, I witnessed the incredible power teachers have to change lives and the awe-inspiring potential students have to change the world.

As a Law Student

At Georgetown Law Center I earned the position of Senior Online Content Editor for the *Georgetown Journal of International Law Online: The Summit*. It was a rewarding position that fed my love of research and writing about global issues. However, I was more than thrilled and humbled to read this email greeting: Congratulations! You have been accepted to the International Women's Human Rights Clinic for the Fall 2015 semester. Only eight students are selected per semester, and I was one of them! As a Spelman alumna, my advocacy for women is unwavering, and it was reinforced through my travels as a Spelman student. This unique learning experience positioned a law student to learn important skills and techniques by working with actual clients: girls and women whose human rights are being violated. The International Women's Human Rights Clinic provided an avenue through which I deepened and enriched my knowledge base and simultaneously molded me as a more effective servant leader.

As a Law Professional

Upon graduation from Georgetown, I joined a law firm with offices in the Americas, Europe, and Asia. In 2020, I had the opportunity to travel to South Africa for a week to work with clients. Again, I was able to make the trip, work, and live with relative comfort because of the global mindset and exposure that Spelman sees as a critical part of the learning process.

As a Tourist

Not only has travel shaped my voice and cultivated a passion for global diplomacy and justice, it also is my favorite pastime. To date, I have visited over ten countries and two continents. Travel is one of the best teachers. To that end, I endorse Dr. Martin Luther King Jr.'s assertion on education. He believed that "education has a two-fold function to perform in the life of man and in society: the one is utility and the other is culture." And so it is with travel!

About the Author

Courtney C. Cox '12 suddenly and tragically passed away in Atlanta on October 20. Currently, a memorial scholarship is being created in her honor for Women in International Law. This essay was forwarded to her mother, Barbara Mebane, EdD to edit. "Courtney was passionate about traveling the world," says Barbara. For contact, bamebane@prodigy.net

Chapter Twenty-Two

Studying Abroad in Jamaica

Dionne C. Griffiths

Spelman College, USA

I was born and raised in the United States. My mother is African American and my father is a naturalized U.S. citizen born and raised in Jamaica. And I proudly identify as both African American and Jamaican. Growing up, I mainly learned about Jamaican culture from my Jamaican grandmother who visited us in the United States every few years in the summer. During my youth, I traveled to Jamaica with my family a few times and we stayed at my grandmother's house. The longest I had ever been in Jamaica was a week and it was mainly in Kingston, the capital. So, I wanted to learn more about the history and culture of Jamaica by living and studying there for an academic year.

As a Spelman College junior, I studied abroad in Jamaica for the academic year 1999 – 2000. I was fortunate to receive the Merrill Travel Abroad scholarship as well. I attended the University of the West Indies – Mona campus (UWI) and I took additional classes at the Edna Manley College of Visual and Performing Arts.

Studying abroad in Jamaica was a pivotal experience for me. I lived on campus in Mary Seacole Hall, the all-female dorm. And I was very active in campus activities, such as being a member of the University Dance Society, which was an audition-based dance performance ensemble. Some of the dance instructors included members of the National Dance Theatre Company of Jamaica (NDTC), the founder of L'Acadco, and independent choreographers. In this ensemble, I grew as a dancer and performer and found a community.

I was also a committee member and contributing writer for Mary Seacole Hall's literary magazine, *Oasis*, which published an annual magazine in the second semester. By serving on this committee, I gained a deeper appreciation for the Mary Seacole Hall staff, the vendors, and the students. It was a collaborative experience compiling students' poems, conducting interviews, taking photographs, having meetings, and creating the final product. In my first week on campus, I was also selected as the D-Block Publication Secretary for my dorm. That vote of confidence from the young women in my dorm gave me the reassurance that I could authentically pursue my academic and extracurricular interests at UWI with success.

Since I was a Comparative Women's Studies major and dance minor at Spelman, I pursued related courses at UWI. Some of the classes I took included West Indian Poetry and Francophone Women Writers. I gained so much knowledge about the diversity, complexity, and beauty of Caribbean literature and gender roles in the Caribbean. The courses also broadened my worldview and deepened my love of literature by authors of African descent.

The Jamaican folk dance class and Jamaican culture class that I took at the Edna Manley College connected me more deeply to my cultural roots in ways I would not have experienced elsewhere. I learned dances such as Dinki Mini, Bruckins, and Jonkunnu. These dances served as a part of funeral rites, represented emancipation from slavery, and were a masquerade celebration during Christmas, respectively. Through these dance classes, I physically embodied the cultural dances that were significant to my Jamaican ancestors for centuries. With bare feet, sweat, and breath, I connected to the drums and the wind instruments, as we shuffled our feet, shifted our hips, and rocked with our arms. I was home in the movement. Also, I had the wonderful opportunity of dancing alongside Jamaican young adults and building a rapport with them.

While studying abroad, I also learned Jamaican Patois. The student population was primarily Caribbean with the majority being Jamaican students. (Other students came from places like Belize, The Bahamas, St. Kitts & Nevis, and Trinidad, for example.) I learned Jamaican Patois in social conversations with students from our "brother dorm", Chancellor Hall. Occasionally during meetings, the student leaders of the University Dance Society and Mary Seacole Hall D-Block would speak emphatically in Patois. As a result, I learned to piece together what they were saying by filling in the blanks of the words I did not know and understanding the context of the discussion. Learning and understanding Jamaican Patois made me feel more immersed in the country, culture, and university community.

Before I studied abroad in Jamaica, I did not really know how to cook. I only knew how to boil water. At UWI we had full kitchens in our dorms and we were expected to grocery shop and cook for ourselves. There was no meal plan. Although there was a cafeteria at my dorm, it was mainly patronized by commuter students, faculty, and staff. Sometimes, I would go there to buy a quick lunch of a cheese pie or callaloo pie and box juice. Or I would occasionally get my favorite fried dumplings and scrambled eggs on a Saturday morning. Otherwise, I knew it was my responsibility to cook on my own. Buying cafeteria meals would add up after a while. So, I ate Kraft macaroni and cheese and spaghetti pasta with Ragu sauce for lunch and dinner, and I ate cereal for breakfast.

I eventually learned how to cook rice after asking one of the young women on my floor to teach me. That expanded the variety of meals I could create and I was very thankful to her. One night, I was still very famished and did not have much food in my dorm room. The cafeteria and tuck shop were closed. And we did not have a vending machine in our dorm yet. So, I went to another young woman in my dorm and let her know I was hungry and didn't have anything to cook. She was compassionate and gave me a can of her sardines. She was like a big sister to me and her generosity helped fill my stomach for a night and filled my heart for a lifetime. When my mother mailed me an Easter care package, I shared the holiday candy with the surprised young women on my floor. Being a student at UWI and living on campus reiterated interdependence.

As an exchange student, I recognized that some people will perceive an American abroad as being representative of whoever the American president is at the time and whatever the American policies are at that time. I remember telling a Jamaican-Canadian student, "I am not the U.S. president. And I *didn't* vote for him." She replied, "But that's your government!" I knew not to get into political or religious debates while abroad, based on my study abroad orientation. So, I shook my head and let the conversation subside.

Studying abroad also gave me the priceless opportunity of speaking to and seeing my granduncle Redmond, my grandmother's youngest brother. My grandma Ivy died the year before and I did not have the opportunity to attend her funeral. So, it was a blessing to connect with my relative, and talk on the phone, and visit him a few times at his home in Kingston.

I also spent time with my godmother Stella, godfather Audley, and godsister Mariel who lived in Jamaica during that time. They picked me up from the airport and helped me get settled into my dorm. Their home was also my refuge when the water was shut off on campus for a day or two one weekend. I did not recognize my privilege at that time. However, I leaned on this resource sparingly, knowing my godparents had their own lives, and that I should confront any campus life challenge like any of the Caribbean students.

Studying abroad in Jamaica for an academic year connected me more deeply to my Jamaican cultural identity, the land of some of my ancestors, and the history of the country. It made me keenly aware of being able to differentiate between cultural norms and practices versus an individual's personal beliefs and ways of being.

Also, I learned to be more gracious to others while in a foreign country even if my ancestors and living relatives are from that country, because I understand that I will be seen as a foreigner by some or a long-lost daughter of the soil by others. I learned you can get an outstanding education in a Caribbean country, but I never doubted that. I learned that Jamaica's most valuable resource is its people and the knowledge, history, culture, and creativity they have to share.

My study abroad experience in Jamaica, and being an exchange student to Brazil for six weeks in high school and later being a Fulbright Fellow to Trinidad (2006 – 2007), strengthened my leadership skills, perseverance, and my resourcefulness. These experiences taught me the importance of cultural humility, interpersonal communication, and the complexity of humanity. They gave me the chance to build cross-cultural bridges. As a Black American woman, studying abroad afforded me the opportunity to be a positive role model for Black women in other countries who are marginalized because of their color, class, gender, or level of educational attainment. I am eternally grateful for those opportunities.

About the Author

Dionne C. Griffiths graduated Magna Cum Laude and Phi Beta Kappa with her Bachelor of Arts in Comparative Women's Studies and minor in Dance from Spelman College. She earned her Master of Arts in Choreography from the University of North Carolina – Greensboro and she was a Fulbright Fellow to Trinidad where she researched, choreographed, and performed dance. Dionne earned her Master of Science in Business Communication from Spalding University and she is a Community Leadership Officer at a philanthropic organization in Indianapolis, IN. Email: Dionne.Griffiths@gmail.com

Chapter Twenty-Three

Coming From Japan

My New Experiences

Anetha Evans

Spelman College, USA

I was seven years old when I was told that my family and I would be moving to Okinawa, Japan. Living in California, I did not know much about Okinawa at the time, but I was extremely enthusiastic to live in a place I never had before, and my parents added to my excitement by introducing me to how people live in Japan once we moved. Differences like the driver being on the right side of the car, speaking common phrases in Japanese, and trips all around the island only further grasped my curiosity. In school, I took as many Japanese-related classes as I could, learned how to write my name in Japanese, and immersed myself in cultural activities. My dad's orders lasted three years, and once it was time for him to change stations, I had to say goodbye to living in Okinawa. Deep down, I knew that I would be back some day, for I longed to experience more of Japan.

Seven years later, I was enjoying the summer of my third year of high school in Alexandria, Virginia. I had spent middle school in Beaufort, South Carolina, and already had readjusted to living in America when my dad approached my brother and me. At this time, my dad was a Major in the Marine Corps, and we already understood that every three years, my family moved somewhere new. The catch was that I was going into my senior year, and my brother, a rising junior, was not far behind. My dad vocalized his concerns about my brother and me graduating high school, and said that he had two options: look for a two-year extension, so that my brother and I could graduate in the same school, or move back to Japan during the upcoming year. While I greatly appreciated his thoughtfulness, I also knew that I would jump at the chance to live somewhere different, even if I had already experienced a part of it.

As time went by, we arrived back in Okinawa for my senior year of high school. After graduation, I left Japan in order to attend Spelman College, but the Spring 2020 closure due to the Coronavirus pandemic led to my return to Japan. This time around, I studied more Japanese, worked as an apprentice glassblower alongside native Japanese speakers, and immersed myself even more into the language and culture of Okinawa, Japan.

Every time I went off-base, I would challenge myself to speak only in Japanese. While doing so earned me the title of "translator" by my family, working in a Japanese environment taught me that I still had a lot to learn. In November of 2020, I tagged along with my mom and her friends to UMIKAZE, a glass works place where customers can buy glass and try their hand at Ryukyu glassblowing. From the moment we entered the factory, I was conversing with the staff and the glass blowers, asking them questions regarding Ryukyu glassblowing and the process. As an experimental and versatile artist, I love to experience various forms of art. Taking part in making my glass enchanted me, and at the end of our experience, I asked if I would be able to work there as an apprentice glassblower.

I didn't fully acknowledge the possibility that none of my coworkers could speak fluent English, and I myself wasn't fluent in Japanese when I began to work as an apprentice glassblower. The first several days were exhausting in the sense that I had to learn both glassblowing and common workplace terminology in Japanese. Furthermore, everything was labeled in Japanese, and I was taught how to blow glass in a language that I was still learning. Many conversations fizzled out because I struggled to convey my intentions in Japanese. Over the next few months, I continued to work and learn, I picked up on key words and phrases, and also grew accustomed to how each of my coworkers spoke Japanese.

After working at the glass works for 7 months, my final workdays held some of the smoothest conversations, and I learned how to understand Japanese beyond what I was taught in a textbook.

My biggest challenge was learning how to understand native Japanese speech. Like in English, sometimes words and phrases are shortened or pushed together, and depending on the situation, informal speech is preferred. While I lived in Okinawa for six years, I focused a lot of my Japanese comprehension towards studying on my own. By doing so, I had a level foundation for how I speak Japanese, recognize the characters that I drew, and how I understand Japanese. My initial approach to learning Japanese overshadowed the most important factor when learning a foreign language: effective communication. Although I may speak clearly, I was only able to comprehend when things were spoken to me with straight annunciation. It wasn't until last year that I altered my approach to learning Japanese, and once that occurred, I began to refine my conversational skills. Now, I can sift through dialogues and understand the messages they convey.

On a personal note, I love learning about Japan's culture and language. Immersing myself in the language and the arts that surround Japan influenced me to minor in Japan Studies at Spelman College. Out of all of the places in which I've lived, Okinawa, Japan stands as one of the few places I've longed to return again. For this reason, I claim Okinawa as my hometown. Because of my father's profession, my family and I were able to engage in cross-cultural experiences that expanded our perspective on the world in which we live.

The image above is a sample of the various kinds of glass made at UMIKAZE Ryukyu Glass Works.

As an apprentice, I assisted in transferring the glass, organizing the designs, preparing the glass materials, adding the logo, and other tasks that were asked of me. Over time, I grew to complete more tasks.

During my Spring 2020 semester, Spelman College was closed, resulting in students and faculty alike returning to their place of residence. I traveled nearly 8,000 miles back to Japan, where I was met with succeeding college semesters that took a harsher toll on my livelihood in comparison to being a student on Spelman's campus. The 13/14-hour time zone difference changed my 08:00-18:15 class schedule to 21:00-07:15. In order to adapt to my new schedule, I slept throughout my days, and stayed up all night. Of course, this routine had its obstacles. There were a handful of days where exhaustion took over and I would sleep through my classes, especially if I attempted to take a nap before classes would begin. When I started working in December, my sleep schedule was gradually compressed. I took into consideration how working and taking online classes placed a strain on my body, so I organized my course schedule to accommodate for my job and the time zone. Ideally, my day would start with work at 08:30 and end at 17:00. I would get some rest before starting classes at 23:00, and running until around 05:00.

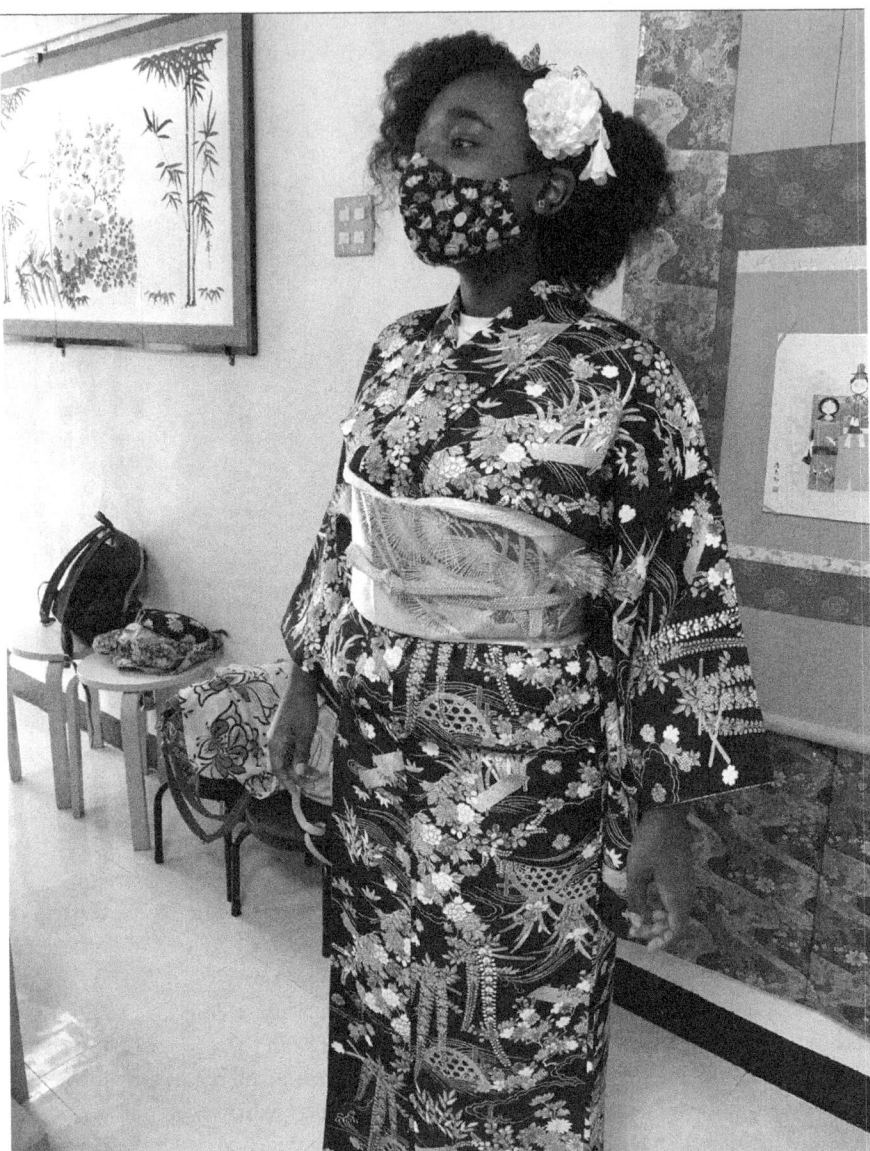

This was the kimono I wore during the tea ceremony

The image above was taken during a tea ceremony experience. While enjoying the experience, I was practicing my skills in Japanese and learning about how to conduct a proper tea ceremony in Japan.

All in all, living in Okinawa has given me many joys and some troubles. During my time living there, the Okinawans encouraged me to speak Japanese, and expressed their joy and support of my efforts. Every time that I went off-base, I was greeted with engaging activities like *ikebana* (Japanese flower arrangement), tea ceremonies, and *bingata* (a form of fabric dyeing). Being able to look out my window and see the glistening ocean was beautiful, and the marine life freshly caught from the waters tasted amazing as well. I explored the island whenever I had the chance, and became enthralled by the scenery, people, culture, and language. While it was only temporary, Okinawa left a major impact on my life.

About the Author

Anetha Evans is a third-year Art major, Japan Studies minor, and Interactive Media minor at Spelman College. Due to her father's service to the Marine Corps, she and her family have lived in various locations throughout her life. After living in Japan for six years, Ms. Evans claims Okinawa to be her hometown. She is currently exploring a plethora of activities while in college. As the President of Japan Club and a member of several other organizations, Ms. Evans spends her time creating visual artworks, developing an app, working to be an assistant director for a dramedy web series, and selling her first published Japanese-manga style graphic novel. Email: agevans201@gmail.com

Chapter Twenty-Four

The Spiritual Path to Spain

Christa E. Sanders

Webster University, Accra, Ghana

During the fall of 1989, I entered my sophomore year at *Spelman College*. Coming from a modest, suburban and predominately White town outside of Philadelphia, attending an *HBCU* was a transformative experience. Immersed amongst the *crème de le creme* of Black excellence, my entrance to *Spelman* was a dream come true. A quaint campus with a close-knit community, after just a few weeks, I had already developed lifelong friendships and was beginning to understand the true meaning of sisterhood. I declared a double major in Spanish and Psychology and set my mind on becoming a bilingual therapist. Having visited Spanish speaking countries such as Mexico and the Dominican Republic in high school, I was eager to embark upon a semester abroad in Spain. Approaching the Office of Study Abroad to commence the application process, little did I know in just a few weeks into my sophomore year, my life would change forever.

In late September, I received a phone call from my father. His voice trembled as he shared news that my mother was not doing very well. I was quite anxious, however my father encouraged me to remain in school and focus on my studies. My mother echoed similar sentiments when I spoke to her, compelling me to remain in Atlanta and make plans to reunite with my family over Thanksgiving. A few days shy of the holiday, I returned home to find that my mother's condition had significantly deteriorated. She now had difficulty breathing and was connected to a mobile oxygen tank. I was floored at the sight of my precious mother, previously full of energy, as she now appeared frail and struggled to breathe. Welcoming me home with a warm embrace, she excitedly queried me about school and my plans to study abroad. My mother had always been keen on the idea of a study venture overseas and encouraged me to submit my application immediately. The next day, as my family sat down to enjoy a scrumptious Thanksgiving meal, I was unaware that my mother's days were numbered. I can still remember the feeling of deep gratitude I felt for my family that fateful afternoon. On Sunday, I departed for the airport with my father to return to school. As he escorted me towards the car, I gazed back at my beloved mother standing alone at the door. Tears filled my eyes, as my stomach tied into multiple knots, not fully grasping that this might be our last meeting. Mom waved joyfully and said, "Don't worry about me … Just study hard and let's get you over there to Spain!" Having her parting words close to my heart, I returned to Spelman determined to finish the term successfully with the reassurance that I would return home once again for the Christmas holidays. Unfortunately, less than two weeks later, my sweet mother, at the tender age of 45, joined the ancestors. My life from that very moment was never quite the same.

Springtime eventually approached and I embarked upon an arduous journey of healing as I attempted to unpack my grief. Fortunately, through the college's counseling services, the unyielding support of my Spelman sisters and the steadfast presence and love of my college roommate, I miraculously made it through the semester. During this time, I also received the news I had so long awaited… I had been accepted to Syracuse University's study abroad program in Madrid, Spain! As my eyes glossed over the acceptance letter, tears rolled down my cheeks as I thought of my late mother and her parting words. While her untimely death had spun me into a state of depression, it would be study abroad that would uplift my spirits, and, ultimately, save me. Studying abroad would open my eyes to a brand-new world and restore a sense of much needed peace, calm and hope for a brighter future….

I arrived in Madrid's Barajas International Airport on a scorching hot Sunday afternoon in August. I found myself in a daze as I peered through the crowd of arriving passengers. An orchestra of Spanish accents could be heard from every corner. A friendly young woman in a t-shirt with a Spanish flag approached me and said, *"Bienvenidos a Espana!,"* She then hurriedly beckoned me along with other study abroad participants towards the airport's exit. Following the program leader with our luggage carts in a winding queue, we offloaded our bags and boarded the chartered bus. At that moment, I realized I was the only Spelmanite in the group accompanied by one of my Morehouse brothers. We would keep a watchful eye on each other for the remainder of that semester due to the lasting "SpelHouse" bond we had developed during the early days of our freshman year at the Atlanta University Center (AUC). We were unaware at that moment that we would also form cherished, lasting ties with our fellow study abroad peers during that impactful fall semester.

We embarked upon a two-week journey as part of our orientation to Spain, a memorable voyage and introduction to the rich culture, language, history and traditions of the country. We explored historical sites in eminent cities such as Cordoba, Sevilla and Granada. In those early weeks, we were fully immersed. We explored the impressive Islamic influenced architecture of the majestic Alhambra and the winding cathedral dotted streets and historic Jewish quarters of Sevilla. The country was simply magical.

Christa E. Sanders with father, Dr. Boykin Sanders in Madrid, Spain.

It was intriguing to see how the blend of Christian, Jewish and Islamic influences had shaped modern day Spain. Taking in the captivating landscape, amidst sampling world-renowned vino tinto and tapas, the experience felt like a dream. As the semester progressed, we would also visit the famous architect, Antoni Gaudi's awe-inspiring cathedral, La Basílica de la Sagrada Familia and witness Salvador Dali's outlandish, surrealist paintings in Barcelona. Today, these pivotal moments remain permanently etched in my mind.

When we returned from orientation, I was assigned a roommate and we were matched with a Spanish host family in a bustling neighborhood of Madrid, near the popular Plaza del Sol. Our host brothers, Luis and Jose, their spirited mother, Ana, and their cat, "Gato," would soon become family to us. Compelled to speak Spanish daily, our communication skills advanced as we navigated the city, indulging in the many pleasures of life as Madrilenos. Ana taught us how to prepare mouthwatering Spanish meals from *tortilla* (an omelet made with potatoes) to the country's national dish, *paella*. On weekends, our brothers would take us out on the town to experience the best of *la marcha* (nightlife) and in the early hours of the morning, we would consume *tazas de chocolate y churros* (cups of hot chocolate and fried dough/donut). Interacting in Spanish daily increased my self-confidence and opened my world to the various idioms of the Spanish language.

Having been sheltered in the suburbs throughout my early life and protected by Spelman's gates my freshman and sophomore years, in Spain I quickly became a mature and confident young woman, not afraid to take on the world. I developed strong cross-cultural bonds with my host family and cultivated meaningful friendships with Spaniards. I became conversant in Cervante's, Don Quijote and, visited the world famous El Museo Nacional del Prado, witnessing the grandeur of Picasso's celebrated "Guernica" for the first time. In just one semester, I transformed; widening my lense of understanding, not only about Spain, but the world at large. As I ventured through a labyrinth of cities and towns across the Spanish peninsula, I also lit candles in remembrance of my mother at every religious site I visited. Lighting candles symbolized a reigniting of her spirit, which kept me connected to her throughout my journey. This was a time of great adventure, self-discovery and learning. Study abroad became an integral part of my development as a young woman, who had experienced unimaginable grief at a tender age.

In retrospect, studying outside of my comfort zone in the United States, molded me personally, spiritually and professionally. The experience left me yearning for more knowledge, cross-cultural exchanges and international educational experiences. Since being in Spain, I have been blessed to travel to over 60 countries and worked in four. The combination of my various experiences has also sparked my interest in Africa, given my travels to North Africa and many interactions with Moroccans while living in Madrid. It is these unique experiences which molded my outlook as well as my current career path. Furthermore, it is my semester abroad in Spain, which jump-started my path towards becoming a global citizen. I am grateful to my dear mother for encouraging me to be bold, daring me to dream, and encouraging me to venture abroad to make my mark. Today, I often reflect on Spelman's current motto, *A Choice to Change the World* and how so many women like myself have been given the special opportunity to study abroad. My beloved Spelman truly showed me that I am capable of changing the world and making an impact in society, with my mother's eternal spirit guiding my path along the way.

About the Author

Christa Elise Sanders is currently the appointed head of Webster University's Ghana Campus in Accra. She has been based in Ghana for the last 17 years where she first helped build *New York University's* first study abroad location in Africa. Christa has also worked in the field of international education in other countries such as Spain, Germany and Ethiopia. She is a consultant and co-founder of *Black Women Abroad* and, furthermore, co-established the *SASS! Study Abroad Student Scholarship* program for Spelman women interested in study opportunities in Africa and the world at large.

Chapter Twenty-Five

Where I'm From

Munobva Kupi

Keshia Abraham

Spleman College, USA

"Where am I from? Pittsburgh... no not Philly, Pittsburgh, you know, like the Steelers?" As a first semester freshman at Spelman, I must have said this phrase over fifty times as I came to learn a personalized version of the African diaspora through the languages, styles, cadences, swag and not swag our sisters and brothers brought to the Atlanta University Center from cities and country towns all over the world. Of course I now know my "from" as the African diaspora, but to a Pittsburgher to be mistaken for a person from Philadelphia seemed like such an insult in those days. We had so little understanding of the complexities of our identities as first year students finding our way together. As worldly as I thought I was, people repped places I'd never heard of before with conviction. City monikers were added to people's names such that "Charmagne from Birmingham" and "Sharyn from Jersey," carried the reputations of those cities with them. We were never far from the people and places that raised us, and it mattered that these sites of pseudo-belonging be respected. Although I'd traveled domestically and internationally prior to finding myself at home at Spelman, I had never seen or imagined so many different varieties of Blackness in one place before. This bold, vibrant, myriad Blackness was something to marvel at daily in the AUC and something that fascinated me in every class, as I walked around campus and as I found my way around Atlanta. Getting to learn so many variations of who we are both expanded my sense of our culture and made me even more invested in global learning in and about the African diaspora. At Spelman, I processed ways of knowing myself in community with others that required some of the same skills that helped me navigate life as an African American girl without her parents, in high school in Ivrea, Italy, where no one in the village had ever met anyone of my background/ culture/ heritage, and where no one seemed to have imagined an American Black.

When I got to Kutama village, several hours outside of Harare, Zimbabwe, for our rural homestay during the Scripps-Pitzer semester abroad, I hadn't considered that I would be just as foreign here as I was in Northern Italy. Although I'd been deeply dedicated to learning everything I could about Southern African culture through literature, I hadn't considered until I arrived that I, that we, might not live in the imagination of the people here either- not in the village or in town... or that I could be so foreign in Africa. When I write this now, after having lived and worked throughout Southern Africa, South America, Europe, the Caribbean and parts of Asia as an international educator for the better part of thirty years, I realize that both the expectation of feeling at "home," the desire to have one's home known, and testing the boundaries of belonging is likely the most liberating thing studying abroad has given me. Learning about Black liberation and literature in a country twenty years into the process of remaking itself ideally in its own image, among all male classmates at the University of Zimbabwe, enhanced my understanding of Black feminisms, colonialism, education and privilege. Here I got to see our people, the people my parents and Spelman faculty insisted we learn about, as icons for change and harbingers for a freedom that was so much bigger than we knew to imagine at that time. Studying abroad in Southern Africa helped me better understand the world did not inherently know us and gave me a sense of duty to change this.

In Shona I was asked, "Munobva kupi"... I stared. Louder a second time... an elder asked intently, "munobva kupi?" Since we were at the introduction stage of greeting each other I took a chance and hesitantly offered, "Pittsburgh?" Perplexed, the wrinkles on her brow tripled. She walked away and brought someone else over to translate. "Munobva kupi," again but this time slower. Then the newly appointed translator asked, "where are you from... Here when we ask that we mean your lineage. Who are your ancestors? Where do they come from? What came before Pittsburgh?" At that time, having spent maybe two days in Zimbabwe I was utterly unprepared to respond in any sensible way – sensible to the community I had come to live with or sensible for myself. I had no tools for explaining who I am, who I was, who we were... To be grown, or think I was at 19, to have traveled freely about the world for years already and suddenly realize that I had no answer to what was the most basic yet most important question left me utterly sick, anxious, lost, confused, angry, and a slew of other emotions that would come and go for years until I learned to find joy in belonging... everywhere...

Where are you from? Munobva Kupi.... In Shona culture one of the first things I learned was the significance of following the flow, the give and take of the call and response patterns of conversations with elders regardless of the angst of knowing that no matter how truthful or direct an answer I provided, it was still anathema to this space, to this way of knowing to whom one belonged. Here, in Zimbabwe, people ask and can answer with certainty, "I am (a) Mutambira. We come from Rusape, in Manicaland, near Mutare." When it's my turn, "I am an Abraham, I was born in Pittsburgh, Pennsylvania, in the US, my mother is from New York, my father is from Pittsburgh..." and then inevitably the follow up for clarification, "Yes, but where are you really from"? "Where are you people from?" "Who are your people?"

During Spring Break, my Spelman sister and I decided to travel from Zimbabwe to Durban, South Africa, where we had both dreamed of studying abroad but were unable to due to apartheid which was still in the early stages of being dismantled. We stayed in a hotel with white privilege, brown front of house staff and Black people working behind closed doors. On the first day there we went to take a walk on the beach and literally walked right into a dear friend of mine from high school, from Pittsburgh–a home that no longer fit all of the parts of me. Standing there between Chuck, my high school friend and Piper, my Spelman sister, I knew that my sense of home, my sense of "from" was growing, shifting, expanding such that there was an awareness of being part of this land too; a sense that Southern Africa in a way that had gotten inside of me. A soul connection.... In Durban, whenever people asked where I came from I said Zimbabwe, meaning where I literally traveled there from, and several times white Rhodesians and South Africans corrected me by refusing to accept the name Zimbabwe, referring to this free country by its colonial name, Rhodesia, as if they could will away Black independence altogether by simply refusing to say it's name. I remember being both appalled and intrigued by such blatant Afrophobia that could stand in my face and tell me that this magical place that was teaching me so much about life, land, history and culture was a threat to a belief system my passport was supposed to put me in solidarity with. While I literally meant I was coming from Zimbabwe geographically, in the face of such assertions that attempted to divide Black America and Black Southern Africa, I might have felt the most "African" I'd ever felt in my young life. By this time, I'd watched and learned and listened to enough of our elders to know and feel prepared to defend the reality that while we may not be culturally identical like twins, there is no denying that we are family/ cousins.

Everywhere I've gone since–Brazil, Cuba, Senegal, London, Jamaica, Trinidad–every time I have been asked about my "from," I try out a new answer or a different nuance and in just about every place I've been I've met a Spelman woman who has reminded me that amongst us is a home like none other and a "from" that unites us.

Studying abroad made me feel at home in the world. Spelman made me feel at home in myself. Spelman provided me with opportunities to see myself in the world, more specifically in the Black world.. To see and feel myself as a woman in a community of other women coming to know, appreciate and understand our Blackness in the world with pride and clarity. Because of the opportunity to prepare for and study abroad with Dr. Beverly Guy Sheftall, Dr. Gloria Wade Gayles, Professors Judy Gebre Hiwet, Siga Jagne, and Soraya Makerta and Sister President Johnetta Cole we got to experience global learning and living through art, literature, language, and theory offered in ways that allowed us to come know ourselves as women "from Spelman" which is to be women of the world.

Piper Kendrix and Keshia Abraham % '90 in Kutama at Kutama Boys School.

Chapter Twenty-Six

Like You

Avi Walker

Spelman College, USA

"Traveling – it leaves you speechless, then turns you into a storyteller." – **Ibn Battuta**

Although travel was not new to my family, Spelman marked a turning point. The journey through matriculation would fortify and embolden me for the adventures that lay ahead.

I was in my senior year of college when my Spanish professor, during an otherwise innocuous conversation, introduced the idea of studying abroad. I had traveled with my parents of course, but those trips were local and accompanied. In my mind, I had never really traveled, as in a trip abroad without them, and upon that realization, the idea of studying abroad seized hold of me. As my professor went on, my imagination flowed. South America a completely new continent. Then reality hit. It was a summer study abroad that would overlap with graduation, which for most students would not be an issue, but for me a senior, it meant I would not walk across the stage with my class. It was a tough decision, expectation, and convention on the one hand, and on the other hand what seemed like all my aspirations flowing.

I went on to deny myself the opportunity, but in my resolve, I committed in my mind that I would not let such an opportunity pass me again. I walked. I graduated, which would by conventional means mark a successful senior year, the missed opportunity of studying abroad left me unsatisfied. I knew law school was around the corner, and I committed myself to finding such a school that would allow me the same freedom to study abroad as Spelman. My next few years were consumed with the diamond in the rough that drew me back north.

I stood in awe at the tree. Its bark smooth, worn, and weathered. Old. Old and wise. I imagined this tree had seen more than its fair share of travelers like myself, young, old, full of life, new to life, and searching. Searching for something within themselves, or possibly without. Something that would make them feel connected, or something to help them make sense of the world on which they walked.

I was in Cambodia. The jungle overgrown and enveloping the temple which stood before me, a temple my *tuk-tuk* driver had informed me prior to leaving was called *Ta Prohm*. I was in awe. Alone internationally for only the second time in my life, and now on the far-side of the globe. Reflecting, many would have questioned my choice, and in fact several did, but the fire of exploring the world still stuck with me following the missed opportunity with Spelman.

Cambodia would have me for the next week, a brief jaunt from my *actual* study abroad in Tokyo. No, Cambodia and *Siem Reap* specifically were off the beaten path, in more ways than one. I would visit several more temples that day, including the famed Angkor Wat before returning to the deep soaking stone tub of my hotel room. The experience was ethereal. Something of this world, and yet apart. *The tree*, but then too, the place itself. Walking the path of many *Americans* before me, although it was highly unlikely that many looked like me; deeply browned by the constant sun, hair natural with waves turning to lighter browns and ambers. I blended in, which as an afro-Latinx in America is a rarity, and the thought struck me that being black here was like a second-skin or camouflage. *I was free to explore. Free to simply exist.*

Enthralled with the experience, I didn't realize the distance I had trekked; the burning sting of sunburn and heat exhaustion would be kept at bay until the next day, my *actual* birthday. My next brush with *true* freedom wouldn't come for several months.

I booked Indonesia in much the same fashion as my other trips; warm, beach, affordable flights, and accommodations. By this time, my peers too had caught on, and after returning from Cambodia alive, well and ecstatic, they too had begun to venture out on their own travels.

Whereas in Cambodia, I experienced a finite connection with nature, self, and the ancients, Indonesia brought me connection and interconnectedness. I arrived byway of Singapore, and my lodgings here fit more of a hybrid-resort experience. There was a concierge desk, room service, and television. I explored, but I was much more mindful of being a solo female presenting traveler. Public safety's warnings to stay in groups of threes and fours echoed in my head, and for the first few days I truly considered I had bit off more than I could chew. I had booked a longer trip this time, two-and-a-half weeks, and it was more so the idea of wasting money than anything else that pushed me to embrace the environment I was in.

I gradually ventured out. Google Maps was my friend again as I strolled to the beach, walking along the shores after navigating through some residential spaces. The shoreline guided me, the waves beckoning and comforting me with the walk easing both mind and body. Small children playing in the surf. Brown children. Brown children who looked a bit like me. I continued onward. Women selling their wares and *upselling and up charging* the tourists. I peeked into a stall. *Sarongs*. The woman said to me, caressing the material between her palms. She looked at me curiously, as she could see the blank stare on my face and began to elaborate on the many uses. I bought several. I was the upsold, up-charged tourist.

Days passed and I became more comfortable learning my surroundings. Locals in the area would nod or wave, and the store clerk stopped offering me plastic bags at checkout. I continued to walk, and the homesickness began to fade. I had been in Asia nearly four months, but Indonesia had begun to feel less foreign. I was blending again. My brown skin was a blessing.

I walked into another store, continuing my adventure.

"You look like me," she said. I looked quizzically. "Like me," she emphasized. "You are brown like me." *Yes, I am* brown. Brown *like you*.

"Travel isn't always pretty. It isn't always comfortable. Sometimes it hurts, it even breaks your heart. But that's OK. The journey changes you; it should change you. It leaves marks on your memory, on your consciousness, on your heart, and on your body. You take something with you. Hopefully, you leave something good behind." – **Anthony Bourdain**

About the Author

Avi V. Aiken Walker is a native New Yorker, born and raised in the Riverdale section of the Bronx. She went on to receive a Bachelor of Arts with Honors in Political Science at Spelman College, and a Juris Doctor with a Certificate of Trial Advocacy and Litigation from Temple University's Beasley School of Law in Philadelphia, PA. While in law school, she participated in a semester study abroad through Temple University Japan (TUJ) in Tokyo, where she serves on the Board of their diversity, inclusion and engagement program TUJ LEAD. She returned home to the Bronx in 2018 to serve as an Assistant District Attorney in the Narcotics and Gangs Investigative Bureau under New York's first black woman elected to the position of District Attorney, Darcel D. Clark. She currently serves in the Office's General Counsel Division and leads their Property Release Unit, coordinating the Office response for the release or deferment of police department confiscated property to defendants and their attorneys. She credits her love of travel to her parents and their family trips abroad. Outside of law and her travels, you can find Avi spending time with family, friends, and her German Shepherd, Roy.

Chapter Twenty-Seven

An Experience of a Lifetime

My Visit to the Spelman College Art Colony

Angelle Cooper

Spelman College, USA

As a lifelong learner, I am continually looking for opportunities to learn and grow. While some of my searches have ended in the pursuit of formal degrees or certifications, other learning opportunities have been more experiential in nature. In the summer of 2012, my quest to find a first-hand experience that combined my love of travel with the need to get in touch with my creative side, led to a remarkable three-week experience......a stay at the Spelman College Summer Art Colony in Portobelo, Panama.

The Spelman College Summer Art Colony was co-founded in 1997 by Dr. Arturo Lindsay, a Panamanian born artist and former Professor of Art and Art History at the Spelman. It was developed to give participants a chance to live, work, and study at Taller Portobelo, an artist cooperative on the Caribbean coast of the Republic of Panama. Not only did the Taller's (Spanish term for artist's studio) idyllic environment provide inspiration for students and emerging artists, but it also offered residents the opportunity to collaborate with local and internationally renowned artists. Additionally, participants received instruction from a visiting artist, as well as guidance from Professor Lindsay.

While all of the opportunities above were mentioned on the art colony's website and in the brochure, neither really captured all that the experience truly encompassed. For years, Taller Portobelo had been a haven for a diversity of artists. During our stay, we got to exchange ideas and work with artists from Portobelo who had received international recognition for their Congo art, a contemporary art form with folk elements that emerged after the U.S. invasion of Panama. For three weeks, all of us – both local and visiting artists- attended workshops in printmaking, papermaking, encaustics (a medium involving wax fixed with heat), reed weaving and other techniques taught by Imna Arroyo, a distinguished visual artist and Professor of Art at Eastern Connecticut State University. We also interacted with a couple of filmmakers – Miguel Sanchez, whose end product had received accolades at the Sundance Film Festival and Toshi Sakai, who was still developing his concept and looking for feedback. Networking with all of these incredibly creative minds was invaluable.

Add to these experiences the backdrop of Portobelo itself. A village with a rich history, Portobelo (beautiful port) was once a great Spanish port that had a key role in the trade of both goods and slaves. Destroyed many times over the years by wars and plundering, its colonial ruins and fortresses are protected as a Unesco World Heritage Site. The village is also the site of the Festival de Cristo Negro (Black Christ), a spiritual celebration that attracts people from around the world on October 21st each year. Even though it is now a poor fishing village, it has a wealth of history and culture which we had an opportunity to explore. There were also many chances to learn about the flora and fauna of the region during our trips to the beach, boat rides across the Bay of Portobelo and hikes through the rain forest.

The opportunity to immerse yourself in a culture other than your own is an experience everyone should have, but few do. By the time our third week rolled around, we had become part of the community. We were able to navigate the village streets on our own, visit local establishments, and hold conversations or exchange greetings with Portobelo residents (depending upon our level of Spanish). We had eaten many Panamanian dishes, participated in several cultural celebrations, and even attended a Friday night jam session at the home of local musicians who are trying to bring back the Congo music of their ancestors. We travelled to Colon, Professor Lindsay's birthplace, where we visited his aunt and toured the neighborhood where he grew up. We also made two field trips to Panama City, where we toured some of the better known attractions, such as the Panama Canal, the Presidential Palace, and Church of the Golden Door.

By the end of our final week, we had also interacted with local school children. We hosted workshops where we taught many of the same art techniques that we had learned a week or two before. It was very gratifying to see these young students absorb new information and watch the creations that unfolded. It was also rewarding to know that we were able to give something back to those who had made us feel so welcome.

Our stay in Portobelo ended with a joint exhibition that included our artwork and those of the local artists and children. It was followed by a celebration of traditional Congo song and dance, and a lunch reception back at Taller Portobelo. Residents of Portobelo and special invited guests from as far away as Panama City attended this culminating event, which marked the end of our three week learning opportunity. It was the perfect ending.

We had made new connections, and as a result, people who started out as strangers now felt like family.

As I boarded the plane back home the next day, I reflected on our amazing educational experience; an experience from which we had received much more than the promotional materials promised and one that had far surpassed my own personal goals.

I had always wanted to study abroad, but the opportunities and finances weren't as readily available when I attended Spelman. Coupled with my desire to further my artwork – something I had pursued on the side since childhood – this chance of a lifetime turned out to be the perfect fit. While I was not the first alumnae to visit Taller Portobelo, I was the first to go as a student and to participate in everything listed on the syllabus – classes, presentations, community sessions and the final exhibition.

For three weeks, I immersed myself in art and culture and I interacted with students, local artists, and residents. The wealth of experiences I had at the Spelman College Summer Art Colony were immeasurable, unimaginable, and unforgettable.

About the Author

Angelle Cooper is a proud graduate of the Class of 1978. A multi-passionate creative, she was able to pursue her interests and skills in art, writing, travel, culture, and community building during her "experience of a lifetime" in Panama. E-mail: af_cooper@yahoo.com

Chapter Twenty-Eight

My Travel Legacy

Kathryn R. Dungy

Spelman College, USA

As a child, my elders continually asked me the heady question, "What do you want to be your legacy?" I am fortunate to have parents who were delighted to expose my sister and me to diverse people, places, cultures, and languages. I also had the privilege of attending Spelman and having mentors who promoted the international experience. Their legacy was to instill curiosity and compassion for people and places on a global scale. I set off on my first international trip at six months of age and have now visited or lived in over 65 countries and territories. Through this proactive approach, I learned many traditions and ways of being. This legacy of my parents and of Spelman not only instilled in me a yearning to explore racial and ethnic identity, racial consciousness, and class identity in a global context, but also a desire to educate others on the complex intersectionality of race, class, and gender inherent in our social interactions.

I experienced double culture shock during my junior year at Spelman. In the fall of 1989, I was the only student of color [out of 33 participants] on the Associated Colleges of the Midwest (ACM) exchange program in San José, Costa Rica. *That fall, I had the privilege of learning about three cultures - PWI college culture, US outbound exchange culture, Costa Rican culture.* After two years immersed in the HBCU cocoon of Spelman and the Atlanta University Center (AUC), it was a jarring adjustment to the ACM study center's U.S. predominately-white college culture. I was not just an American exchange student; I was a *Black* American exchange student. I quickly realized I was experiencing Costa Rica quite differently than my white counterparts.

ACM staff and Costa Ricans ignored or actively denied the existence of Afro-descendent Costa Ricans admonishing me not to worry about "them." *Real* Tican (term of endearment for a Costa Rican) culture was descendant from Spanish ancestry and was to be found in the highlands and western part of the country. I wanted to spend my mandatory two-week rural stay in the eastern province of Limón along the Caribbean

Sea, where the largest population of Black Costa Ricans resided. However, I had to take the initiative to seek contacts and to engage with the community. I was told: "Well, we had a black girl on our program about three years ago. We told her she couldn't go to Limón and she didn't make a fuss. She had a marvelous stay in Puntarenas province on the Pacific side." I stood my ground and eventually made connections that resulted in a wonderful homestay with a Black Costa Rican family in Limón Province. At the conclusion our homestays, program participants presented reports about our personal immersions int Tican culture. I shared information about an occluded segment of Costa Rican culture and my experience proved eye opening for my entire cohort and for the ACM site directors.

I spent spring of 1990 on a CIEE (Council on International Educational Exchange) program in Santiago de los Caballeros, Dominican Republic; a decidedly different experience than Costa Rica. While I was still one of only two people of color on the program, we were integrated into the local university and took classes alongside Dominican students. The Caribbean culture and the preponderance of Afro Descendant peoples on the island allowed me to blend in better than I had in Costa Rica. One of my favorite memories is of walking down a Santiago street with another program participant. A kid yelled from the window of a passing school bus, "Ah, la Dominicana y la Americana!" I looked around for the pair she was shouting about and only belatedly realized she thought that *I* was Dominican and I was walking around with an American. I carried a double identity simply walking down the street in San José or Santiago. I could pass as a local as long as I didn't open my mouth. Only then would a baffled Tican or Dominican question my origin. The assumption in Costa Rica was that I must be from Limón Province. The assumption in the Dominican Republic was that I was either from another Caribbean island or that I was a Dominican raised in the U.S. who had sadly "lost my culture."

Color prejudice in Latin America is different from the U.S. idea of color prejudice. It is difficult to explain, but once you are in it, you know that the U.S. idea of being Black is totally unlike the Latin American experience. My conceptualization of the social constructs of race and skin color in the United States was profoundly challenged when I discussed my educational experience in these Latin American environments. There was no objection when I mentioned I went to an all-women's college because all-women's institutions are common in Latin America. However, deep discussions ensued when I revealed Spelman was also an all-Black institution. I had to explain and defend, in Spanish, my decision to attend an all-women's historically Black college; it was quite challenging.

I had an argument with one of my Dominican friends about the purpose of Historically Black Colleges and Universities (HBCUs). "You're segregating yourselves, that's stupid!" he declared. I tried to explain the historical reason for their existence and the systemic reasons why they still existed. It challenged my Spanish cognitive and speaking abilities to argue on a subject about which I barley had a vocabulary for in English! He still thought my argument was stupid and I found myself reassesing ideas that I had previously believed indelible. The experience heightened my sensitivity towards myself, towards my country, and towards other nations in the world.

Being an outward-looking U.S. citizen and a life-long learner is my passion. For me, the best intercultural exchanges occur when relaxing into a culture and language different from my U.S. based experiences; a lesson I learned on the banks of the Guadalquivir River in Seville, Spain. I had lived and studied in multiple Spanish-speaking places and had been in Seville for 2 months completing a summer research project in the Spanish archives. However, even in my immersive living experience I avoided social situations. I did not trust my verbal skills. Unlike old books and papers, people talked back! St. John the Baptist day is huge in Seville and my Spanish flatmate invited me on a picnic with her friends. I was celebrating the holiday with the locals, but I was afraid to engage in conversations. My friend finally turned to me and said, "Don't you have anything to share?" Everyone stopped what they were doing and focused on me, manifesting my biggest fear. What if I made a mistake or messed up a verb? I said something. No one laughed. I said something else. Someone responded and lively conversations followed. I realized that everyone understood me and that even my mistakes were learning experiences. By dawn, I was one of the crew and invited on a daytrip to Portugal! The most important lesson I learned was to relax, to trust myself, and to enjoy the experience.

Wanting others to share in these life-altering moments, I actively promote access to international study for historically underserved students in both my professional and personal work. I currently serve on the board of directors for CIEE, one of the international student exchange programs that supported my college year-abroad. Recently, I returned to Spelman to engage with students about how travel abroad could inform their professional paths. The conversations I had in small classroom settings were the highlight of my visit. We spoke intimately about how Black women experience the world outside the United States. I revealed some experiences I'd faced during my exchange programs and later travels abroad that transformed my life and career. Students openly shared their hopes and fears about traveling and living abroad as Black women. Through follow-up communication with one of the students, I later learned that the affirmation of her presence and importance in the international sphere encouraged her to seek opportunities abroad. This outcome to the candid conversations reinforces my commitment to continue outreach that diversifies international exchanges.

Santiago, Dominican Republic, spring 1990 - Kathryn and my Dominican sister

My overseas experiences are a way for me to reassess myself, strengthening my inner thoughts and feelings about being African American, and cultivate my conception of the global idea of Afro-descendent peoples. I grew into the understanding that we, meaning Black African Americans from the United States, are not the only African Americans. The term African American includes everyone of African descent from Argentina to Canada. My study abroad experience led me to a global awakening in which I became conscious of a larger community of Americans and, by extension, a profound connection to the African Diaspora.

The world became an amazing place to explore and I built my academic studies and career around embracing the diversity of humankind. I study and teach about race, class, and gender in the Atlantic World, exploring the concept of freedom in the midst of slave societies in the Caribbean, Latin America, Europe, and the United States. I strive to illuminate the innumerable stories of those who have been occluded from the narrative. In this way, I hope to foster understanding and compassion in the world around us.

About the Author

Kathryn R. Dungy specializes in the study of race, class, and gender in the Atlantic World and is author of The Conceptualization of Race in Colonial Puerto Rico, 1800–1850. She holds a B.A. in History and Sociology from Spelman College, and an M.A. and Ph.D. in History from Duke University. She currently serves as Chair of the Department of History at Saint Michael's College (VT). A world traveler since the age of six months, Dr. Dungy has traveled to over 60 countries and territories and has lived in Nigeria, Puerto Rico, and Spain. In addition, she is an alum of semester study abroad programs in San José, Costa Rica and Santiago de los Caballeros, Dominican Republic and has also spent academic study abroad and research time in Mexico, Puerto Rico, and Spain. She currently serves on the Board of Directors for the Council on International Educational Exchange.

Chapter Twenty-Nine

Unexpected Favor

Mercedes Harris

Spelman College Alumna, United States

I have always been drawn to a myriad of cultures and it may be because my grandfather was a West Indian immigrant. I was also exposed to many Caribbean cultures because I grew up in South Florida. Nevertheless, I love to travel and learn about different ways of life. As a Black American, I have never completely felt at home in the United States and began seeking to live outside of my birth country and immerse myself into a higher level of growth.

The Opportunity

When I joined IBM, I told them that I was interested mainly in the "I" in International Business Machines. I wanted to work overseas. It became the running joke that a 30-year-old single mom would get a role overseas. I was judged immediately and told, that is usually reserved for executives, inferring that I had a long way to go if I was going to be an executive. I kept pushing and within 4 years of joining the company, I accepted an offer to work in Canberra, Australia.

Unwritten Rules

I did not have any expectations of living abroad and felt comfort that I could take my child and mother with me on the journey. The hiring manager prodded me to make sure I would survive the move and insisted that it may be too hard for me and my family. I rebutted that he needed to focus on whether I was the right candidate for the role and let me focus on what is best for my family. I had to accept the 2-year contract offer without a visit and I had never been to Australia. They could have been sending me to the bowels of hell (which a family member said) and I would have no idea. Yet, I jumped in headfirst and tried my best to belong.

A field of tulips in Canberra, Australia

There were very few American black women in the city, outside of American diplomats. Race ended up not being what made me feel alienated. One of my first observations was that many of our social interactions were separated by gender. I would often attend events where women would be on one side of the room and men on the other. I was used to working in a predominately male workforce. I also have several brothers. It was not odd for me to gravitate to talk to men, yet I am comfortable in engaging with women as well.

I noticed that when I would end up in conversations with men, women gave me death stares across the room as if I violated a social contract that I did not sign. In addition, if I went to an event where there were married couples, I would often find a wife swarming within 5 seconds of engaging in a conversation with her spouse. Yet, I was never interested in her partner.

I was talking to anyone that would talk to me. It took a while to recognize that many of the white-collar professionals had gone to same gender schools and were not accustomed to mixing genders socially. I broke the code and did not realize it. I was so accustomed to being placed in a box because of my race, it was the first time where I experienced social discomfort because I was unaware of the social norms between men and women. I was supposed to know my place. My naivety had me walking across lines that I did not know existed. The same thing happened when I realized I was privileged as an American.

Former Netherlands Ambassador Annemieke Ruigrok and Mercedes Harris

American Privilege

Though I am accustomed to gender-based oppression, I was deeply perplexed the first time that I experienced privilege. I would walk into a store while in Canberra, and the shop owner would respond to me with a neutral facial expression with a lean towards negative, until I spoke. The sigh of relief would usually be accompanied by a burst of energy and proclaim, "Oh, you're American." Unbeknownst to them, that added further insult to the injury because even though I was born in America, I never considered myself only American. Yet, that is how I was viewed in Australia (once I spoke).

When I found myself out with "the guys" for drinks one night, I realized that I somehow ended up in a dead-end conversation of racial jokes about Aboriginal people. I could not believe it was happening. Did they not realize that I was also black? I spoke up and the response that I received was, "No, you are one of us."

No, I am not one of you. I will never be one of you. However, reality hit me and knocked me breathless. I, indeed, was experiencing privilege. Had I not been viewing the world from the lens of a black American woman; I may not have been able to recognize that it was a privilege of which I was a beneficiary. The gift that Australia gave me was being able to go back to America with a different perspective.

As a black American, I often cannot comprehend why those that are the beneficiaries of systematic oppression have such a hard time seeing their advantages. Yet, my experience abroad helped me understand how easy it is to choose the road of privilege because it feels great. Why would I want to choose to be mistreated when I get special favors for some attribute that is favored? I now have more empathy with understanding why some people fight so hard to hoard their privilege. In addition, I understand what it feels like for a person to loan their privilege. I did not expect to be treated any differently in Australia than I am treated in America. Yet, I quickly learned that sometimes, I can go places and all they see is where I was born, irrespective of my cultural identity.

About the Author

Mercedes Harris, is a graduate of Spelman College. She majored in Chemistry and Chemical Engineering through the Dual Degree Engineering Program. She is currently working in the technology industry. Email: merlex@hotmail.com

Chapter Thirty

A Journey of Connectedness through Study Abroad Experiences

Virginia Davis Floyd

Spelman College, USA

I am standing at the foot of the Egyptian pyramids. The date is July 19, 2021, and I am remembering my first global experience as a sophomore at Spelman College.. I was a recipient of the Merrill Scholarship, which supported my studies abroad to Sophia University in Tokyo, Japan, in 1971-72.

My advisor and professor, Dr. James Gates, could not understand why I did not want to study in Europe, especially since a Spelman student had never gone to Japan. However, my logic was simple. I could travel to Europe for $500 roundtrip and I wanted to go as far as my scholarship could take me. As a scholarship recipient, the $7000 Merrill Scholarship was a huge amount of money, so much so, before I left for Japan I was able to give some of the scholarship funds to the Spelman tutorial program in Atlanta for the Summerhill Community. With the rest, I purchased an around the world ticket from Atlanta's Black travel agency, Henderson Travel. I packed my bags and headed west.

I inherited this wanderlust from my father,, who joined the Merchant Marines after discrimination kept him and his chemistry degree from Lincoln University out of corporate industry in the 1930s. He made $10,000 a year, and I had just received a $7,000 travel scholarship. I was rich beyond my wildest dreams! As a child, I remember sitting on a log in front of our house waiting for the mailman to bring postcards my father sent from exotic places around the globe. When he returned home, he would tell us stories of his travels in foreign ports of call. It was my father who put me, at the age of sixteen, on my first airplane to visit my brother who was stationed in the Army in Stuttgart, Germany.

It was my father's suggestion that for my Merrill sojourn, I purchase an "around-the-world" ticket because there are so many wonderful places "around the world" to experience. Imagine being able to visit and experience Beijing, Tehran, Cairo, Istanbul; I can hear my father saying, "Ginger, make it a one-way trip heading West, and you will eventually end up back home". Imagine a small-town girl from a segregated New Jersey town of less than 5000 with no stoplight traveling around the world!

The building blocks of my life's foundation during my Spelman experience were enormous, but none more powerful and formative as my year of study in Japan. I remember informing the registrar at Spelman that I did not intend to go to Japan to study more biology, chemistry, or calculus. I had already failed one of those courses at Spelman as a premed major! I was going to Japan to touch, feel, learn, experience, immerse myself in another culture, meet new people, and hear a different song. To that end, my class list included Japanese, ikebana flower arranging, origami, and woodblock printing. I had to convince an elderly Japanese teacher that a nonnative could and should be allowed to become a serious student of ikebana. She finally accepted me as a student, and weekly lessons in her home and guided trips to the local flower market became an authentic immersion experience into a Japanese family and its daily rituals – a part of Japan I could not have experienced as a mere tourist.

I lived in a very small Japanese (tatami floor) apartment with a small oil heater. The winter was very cold! My bath routine consisted of frequent trips to my local neighborhood sentō, a communal bathhouse. While bathing with the local neighborhood women, I finally blended in, and not only did we become familiar with the different body physiques, we accepted the difference because they were insignificant.

Unfortunately, the remainder of that $7000 scholarship did not go as far as I had hoped. I implemented a secondary plan and took a job as an English tutor for Japanese college students who wanted to perfect their English. With that unexpected opportunity, the world of Japan opened up in a whole new expansive way. My students and I traveled throughout the country together, took ski lessons, shared dinners, and attended concerts. The global experience was transformed from wonderful to utterly fantastic.. Although we saw the world through different eyes and cultures, we viewed the world together. We gave each other the tremendous gift of collective, shared learning.

Japan was far away from my little town in New Jersey and the familiar campus of Spelman. Homesickness began to impact my travel abroad experience. Where were the folks who spoke English, ate hamburgers, and listened to Motown? Searching for familiarity, I found my way onto the US Air Force base, Tachikawa, where my premed knowledge was quickly put to work volunteering in a hospital. I had marched against the Vietnam War and proudly wore the peace symbol (even though my older brother served two tours of duty there). This Air Force hospital was the air evacuation site for Vietnam War injuries, and here I saw young men the same age as me returning from the frontlines in pieces both physically and mentally, casted, surgically pinned, and mentally distraught. I learned of "walking point" – being the first in the line and the first to step on the landmine. Foreign bodies and shrapnel surgically removed, bones and bodies pinned together, future dreams shattered, yet I witnessed unbelievable patriotism through these US soldiers' hearts and eyes. My witness deepened my calling to become a doctor. Early entrance to medical school and the need to work to earn tuition ended my "around-the-world" trip. I returned East to Atlanta to prepare for medical school.

Spelman prepared me well for the next stage of my life – becoming a doctor – and off I went to Howard University College of Medicine. Also, my father was the reason for my aspiring to be a doctor and why I became a Spelman student and a world traveler. An ardent believer in HBCUs, and the son of a professor at Tougaloo College, he supported my older sister, also a Spelman alum, as the first in our immediate family to attend college. Always encouraging me to do well -- actually demanding that I do well -- they built in me the internal recognition of my capabilities and the ability to dream and dream big. Becoming a physician was that dream. My father died of cancer three months before he was able to watch me, his baby daughter, walk across the stage to receive her MD degree.

Since Japan, my wanderlust has never stopped. Now thirty-six countries later, full of global health and diplomacy work, international philanthropy, traditional medicine village experiences, vacations, and Spelman Independent Scholars (SIS) global learning trips, I feel the seed planted by my father deepening its roots. My one regret is not being able to thank Spelman College enough for this positive life-changing experience.

Years later, in July 2021, as I stand at the foot of the Egyptian pyramids, I offer a prayer of thanks for the institution that recognized something in me, not seen by myself, that began my global "journey of connectedness," allowing me to learn from this continuous worldwide travel and cultural immersion that we are more alike than different.

I am honored to currently serve as a Visiting Scholar in Traditional Knowledge for the Spelman Independent Scholars (SIS) program. SIS is a unique program that opens the lens of age in research, writing, and global travel. It is the only project at an undergraduate institution in the nation that has published two student-edited anthologies of interviews with African American women who have ranged in age from 73 to 103. Giving back to my alma mater, I have the privilege of co-leading global trips with Dr. Gloria Wade Gayles for our SIS scholars to Ghana, Jamaica, and the Bahamas. Seeing the astonishment in their eyes, hearing the excitement in their voices, and watching the transformation that occurs through the global experience allows me to relive my Spelman Japanese experience. Some things do not change. Learning how to be a responsible and culturally sensitive global citizen is one of them.

During my time at Spelman, the Merrill Scholarship was limited to a small number of students. Today our Spelman Gordon-Zeto Center facilitates global learning experiences for hundreds of our students annually – opening the doors of the world and their minds. A Choice to Change the World, our Spelman tagline, has a special interpretation as Spelman students immerse themselves in countries and cultures worldwide. I know that these experiences will begin an individual Journey of Connectedness for each Spelman student. The experiences will be many – and life-changing.

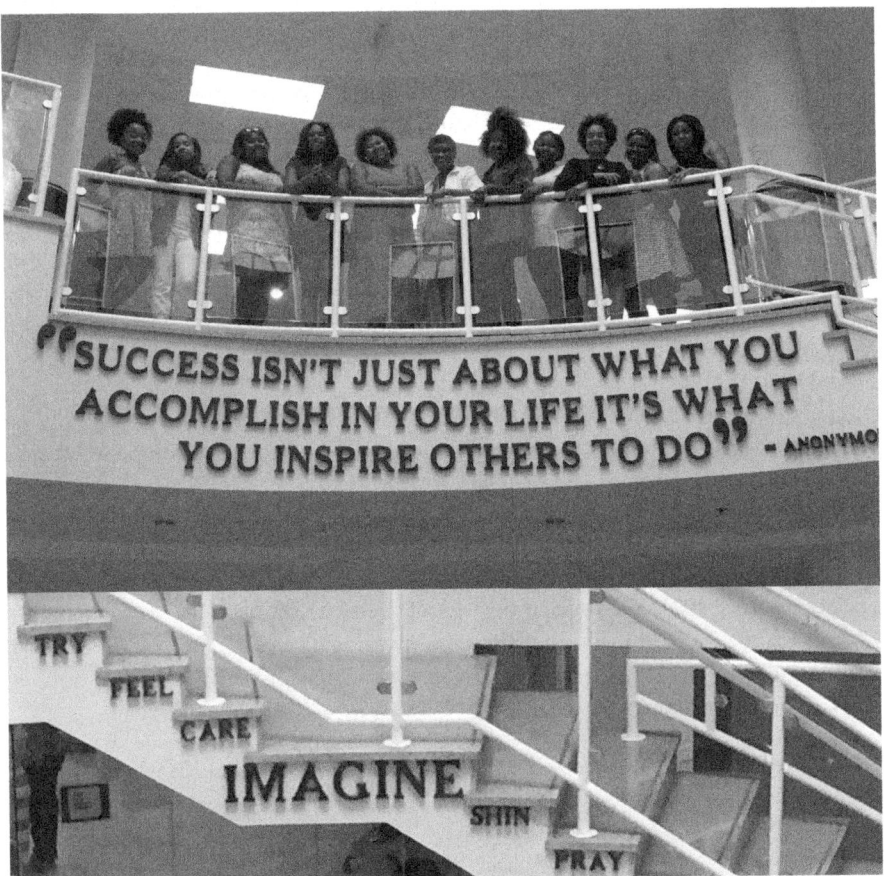

About the Author

Virginia Davis Floyd, MD, MPH, Spelman Class of 1973. Virginia "Ginger" Floyd is a public health physician with research interests in traditional medicine and indigenous science. She is an Associate Professor at the Morehouse School of Medicine and serves as a Visiting Scholar in Traditional Knowledge in the Spelman Independent Scholars (SIS) Program. Emails: virginiafloyd@virginiafloyd.org

Chapter Thirty-One

From Crowdfunding to a Gilman Scholar and Beyond

The Study Abroad Journey of a Low-Income First Generation Student

Aaliyah J. Deggs

Spelman College, USA

As a first-generation college student from a low socioeconomic background, traveling abroad seemed like an unattainable dream. I did not have the access, resources, or capital to engage in global exploration. Spelman College provided multiple opportunities for my far-fetched dream to become a reality. Being in a competitive yet supportive environment like Spelman College helped shape my understanding of the diversity within the United States, the world, and most importantly, myself. Through my journey on the margins, I have accepted that my social class did not define me or limit my college experience.

On March 27, 2015, I attended a Spelman College scholarship banquet. I met two of my scholarship donors, Mary L. Diggs and former Spelman College President, Dr. Beverly Daniel Tatum. As I sat at the table with Dr. Daniel Tatum, I felt out of place because everyone shared about their abroad experience except me. I asked myself, "Am I a true Spelman woman if I don't study abroad?" Even Dr. Daniel Tatum strongly encouraged me to study abroad. I left the scholarship banquet determined to find study abroad opportunities.

Similar to all of my other goals, I created an intentional action plan. First, I talked to the Study Abroad Coordinator to explore programs. During my visit, I was introduced to the Spelman's Independent Scholars (SIS) program, where travel to the Bahamas focused on the importance of oral history. Also, I was encouraged to participate in a Global Education Engagement trip in Havana, Cuba. After meeting with the directors of each program, I chose to attend the Global Education Engagement opportunity in Cuba. The program objectives aligned with my career goals to become an educator. However, this program did not provide any financial support.

With my tenacious attitude, I turned to the crowdfunding option, GoFundMe (GFM). Daily, I shared my GFM link multiple times on all social media platforms. With the support of my community, family, and friends, I met my financial goal. I traveled to Cuba and made Spelman College history by being a member of the first group of students to travel to Cuba. My personalized experience at the Study Abroad Office influenced my decision to apply for a Federal Work-Study job within the office as an Office Assistant. I wanted to provide the same level of support that I received to other Spelmanites.

While in Havana, we explored numerous institutional types: after-school programs, performing arts schools, special schools for students with cognitive needs, and a live homeschooling session. I was intrigued by Cuba's educational system because it prioritized familial collaboration and student needs. At the special schools, parents made lunch for students daily. They understood the correlation between certain foods and behavioral effects, so they removed foods with high sugar content and incorporated more fruits and vegetables. Also, there were small class sizes: two to three students per teacher. Their approach to homeschooling was community-centered and located at a park. There was one teacher, who taught the parents, then the parents immediately taught their children. I loved how students were able to build social skills, which is a common concern with homeschooling in the United States. Both experiences expanded my knowledge of educational approaches. Overall, the entire trip emphasized the importance of community investment and support.

After this experience, I returned to Spelman and my role as an Office Assistant. While conducting inventory of promotional materials for study abroad opportunities, I discovered other programs of interest and financial resources. I decided to apply to a Philosophy and Religious Studies Department trip to Accra, Ghana. This faculty-led abroad opportunity focused on African Indigenous Religion and Culture. As a Sociology and Anthropology major, this month-long experience aligned with my cultural anthropologist lens and my desire to conduct research. This opportunity allowed me to apply for the Benjamin A. Gilman International Scholarship Program. To reduce the financial barriers of studying abroad, the Gilman Scholarship provides financial support to Pell Grant recipients. It was rewarding to know that there was a program that recognized such disparities. Before I applied for the Gilman Scholarship, I relied on crowdfunding again as a supplemental plan. Also, I applied for the Gordon-Zeto & James S. Gates Study Abroad Scholarship. During the Spring 2016, I received communication that I was selected as both a Gordon-Zeto & James S. Gates Memorial recipient and a Gilman scholar. These scholarships allowed me to travel to Accra and conduct research on the oral traditions of the Akan ethnic group within the Fante States.

I am proud that I had the opportunity to travel to two different countries within six months. These experiences inspired me to pursue abroad opportunities after graduation. I applied to the Fulbright U.S. Scholar Program in India and became a semi-finalist. I worked closely with the Office of Study Abroad Director, Dr. Ganz, who continuously encouraged and supported me throughout the process. Although I did not receive the honor of becoming a Fulbright scholar, I am proud I tried and made it that far through the process.

My abroad experiences were developmental and transformative, both personally and professionally. Although cultural immersion was a goal, I learned many soft skills that I still use such as interpersonal skills, problem solving skills, communication skills, adaptability, self-awareness, and agency. Additionally, my travel experiences at Spelman College are the foundation for my career interests in diversifying study abroad. Beyond Spelman College, I entered a two-year master's program and studied abroad each year. During my time in graduate school, I went on to join an organization that creates opportunities abroad for low-income, first-generation, and racially/ethnically minoritized students. I co-presented at a national conference sharing the importance of studying abroad and how to make those experiences affordable.

As a change agent, my role is to encourage students on the margins that they can expand their student engagement opportunities by studying abroad. There are opportunities and resources available to support your journey. I am proof that your socioeconomic background does not define you. Instead, your persistence, determination, resilience, and self-advocacy exemplify your existence.

About the Author

Aaliyah J. Deggs is a Kansas City, Missouri native and Spelman College alumna. While at Spelman College, she earned a B.A. in Sociology and Anthropology. Soon after, she earned an M.A. in Higher Education and a certification in American Indian Higher Education from the University of Arizona in Tucson, Arizona. Currently, she serves as a Residence Life Coordinator at the University of South Florida in Tampa, Florida. As a well-rounded Student Affairs professional, she has worked with diverse college students and supported their personal development and academic success. Email: aaliyahdeggs6@gmail.com

Chapter Thirty-Two

That's the Way of the World

The Soundtrack of a Semester Abroad

Naja Grasty

Spelman College, USA

As I embarked on my 16-hour flight, I wondered what I was getting myself into. Here I was, a student from Spelman which is an HBCU in Atlanta, Georgia, surrounded in my cocoon of Black womanhood, off to Vietnam, where I knew no one and did not speak the language. From the looks of my study abroad Facebook group, I was the only Black person in the program cohort. I carefully packed my suitcase with enough hair products and homemade shea butter to last the duration of the trip, knowing where I would be studying would have nothing to accommodate my needs. I meticulously read articles and watched videos about the experiences of Black people who live in Asia. My friends and family either misunderstood or were elated that I was studying abroad in Vietnam. I mentally prepared myself for the weight of globalized anti-blackness. Despite my rampant feelings of uncertainty, I knew my time abroad would be memorable. While the plane took off, I slipped on my headphones, not knowing how profoundly music would shape my semester abroad.

What's Going on and the Legacy of American Soul

During my semester, I was overwhelmed by the beauty of the natural landscapes of Vietnam. From lush forests to intricate waterways and sprawling countrysides, my academic director made sure we saw all the natural wonders that Vietnam had to offer. Despite being immersed in nature, I searched for a sense of belonging. I remembered being glared at or ignored when I walked into certain rooms. I noticed white expats discontent when seeing me, as Black people were not a part of the colonial fantasies they aimed to live in Vietnam. I had people ask me when my family arrived in America, unsure how to explain slavery to a Vietnamese audience. My hair, skin tone and body were often a topic of discussion. American Soul music kept me company on long bus rides to various excursions throughout Vietnam. Through listening to *What's Going on* by Marvin Gaye, I felt like I reconnected with the ancestors who were casualties in the Vietnam War. While visiting war memorials and monuments, I felt overwhelmed with grief. Music helped me make sense of all that I was experiencing. I was shocked when I learned that *What's Going On* was also a Vietnam war protest song. As I adjusted to my strange new reality, I turned to the legacy of American soul music to help me through this time.

Sisterhood Across Borders

Soon, a few cohort members and staff noticed the difficulties I was experiencing. I moved homestays due to unsavory conditions and missed sleep to communicate with my family back home. I lived vicariously through Instagram posts from friends, torn between feeling grateful for new experiences while clinging to the life I had before. My academic director, Co Thanh, brought me boiled peanuts from a local food stall every morning. The boiled peanuts reminded me of summers in South Carolina and brightened my mornings. She did whatever she could to help me along that semester. My homestay sister Kate stayed up late and listened to my musing on my love of the band Paramore. She shared with me how the music helped her sister get through difficult times as well. While we came from different racial backgrounds, she always did her best and made me feel less bothered due to the rampant anti-blackness I experienced.

My Vietnamese American cohort members, Alicia and Cindy, became my comrades in the struggle. We vented to each other about how white expats made us feel and about the Afro-Asian relations in the United States. We relied on each other as the heat and our cohort members' disrespect of cultural sites became unbearable. We lived together during our program's independent study portion in Ho Chi Minh City. The weekends were spent shopping, and we stayed up late-night eating at the neighborhood Bánh xèo food stall. Every morning, we were awoken by the communist announcement as we lived by the police academy. At night, we fell asleep to the sounds of arguing and karaoke outside of our Airbnb.

One of my favorite memories of my time with my friends was the premiere of the *Beyonce: Homecoming* Coachella concert film. While watching *Homecoming*, I served as a cultural commentator, updating my friends with HBCU facts as we watched when Beyonce came onto the stage and sang "*Lift every Voice and Sing.*" When the Beyonce "Before I Let Go remix" played at the end credits scene, I screamed excitedly as the song is a Black cultural classic. I began sobbing and explained the significance of the music. Even though I was in a hostel in the middle of a rice field, this moment left me with racial pride, and I felt so bound to my people miles and miles away. Later in the evening, I did see messages in the group chat inquiring where the screaming was coming from in the hostel. But for the time being, my white classmates just had to be uncomfortable during my moment of closeness and triumph, and it was the most whole I felt in a long time.

The Land and Sacred Memory

My travels taught me about the resilience of nature and how environments can be sites of sacred memory. When visiting nature trails throughout Vietnam, we were asked not to go off the path as(replace "as" with since) active landmines were still present. As we visited the Mekong Delta, we were amongst mangrove forests that were once completely dissipated by American bombs and had grown back about 40 years later. I spent more time hiking in Vietnam than I ever did in my entire life. Especially (leave out especially) during this time, I tapped heavily into my spirituality. I felt the memories and the past traumas of the land. I was reminded of the black people who drafted to the fight for a country that systematically disenfranchised them. I tried my best to honor their legacy, and not take my experience of traveling to Vietnam as an undergraduate student lightly.

My experience was sullied with anti-blackness and feelings of isolation. I felt like I had something to prove as a Black woman and a woman from Spelman. There were positives in my semester abroad as well; I was able to make valuable connections and walked away with an intense love for Vietnamese food. I also walked away from my experience with a profound respect for community. I would not have made it through without phone calls and texts from friends and family. My community was praying for me and were amazed by the steps of courage it took to study abroad. I had never considered myself a courageous person until after that semester. I learned to treasure both melodies, also silence, and gain reverence for nature.While visiting a monastery, my academic director recommended that I run a meditation exercise with the Buddhist nuns;this was due to meditation skills I cultivated while at Spelman. I learned to surrender and that (delete "and that" and replace with because)running around trying to control everything will lead towards (to instead of towards) self-destruction. As Earth, Wind and Fire said, "Keep your head to the sky; the clouds will tell you why.". As I leaned on music and my newfound connection to nature, I realized I was equipped with tools to make it through.

About the Author

Naja Grasty is a C'2020 graduate of Spelman College. She graduated with a Bachelor of Arts in International Studies with a minor in Comparative Women's Studies. In her junior year, she studied abroad in Ho Chi Minh City, Vietnam, with the School of International Training. Currently, Naja works as a Literacy Tutor at Wexler Grant Elementary School and loves her students dearly. Her primary research interests lie in digital culture, Afro-Asia, Beaty Politics, and globalization, and she plans to pursue graduate study in Socio-Cultural Anthropology. Email: najagrasty113@gmail.com

The STAR Scholars Network is committed to promoting transnational research and collaboration between scholars in different countries (e.g., joint publications and research partnerships) that impacts humanity positively beyond national borders. The Global Connections Awards recognize "STAR Scholars" for their achievements and distinctive contributions to transnational research that demonstrates the very best of scholarship and/or collaboration among scholars around the world in the following categories:

North Star Medal of Lifetime Achievement

Shining Star Research Award

Rising Star Emerging Scholar Award

Star Humanitarian Award

All nominations must include the following:

- Nominator information (i.e., name, email, phone number, title, and affiliation)
- Candidate(s) information (i.e., name or title, email, phone number, and/or affiliation)
- The award category
- A brief bio of the nominee (< 150 words, to be used in promotional material if selected)
- A brief description (< 500 words) of the candidate's contribution to transnational research and why they should receive the specific Global Connections Award

https://starscholars.org/a-noam-chomsky-global-connections-awards/

Recently Published

Edited by Krishna Bista and Anthony L. Pinder

Reimagining Internationalization and International Initiatives at Historically Black Colleges and Universities

"A must-read for all interested in the quality of higher education at an HBCU. Internationalization has long been an integral part of the HBCU history at institutions like Hampton University. This is a timely platform to share the unique ways that the HBCUs have built their institutions on the value of the inclusion of a global population."

—JoAnn W. Haysbert, Chancellor and Provost, *Hampton University, Virginia (USA)*

"This timely book explores the outstanding legacy of global engagement to be found at the nation's historically Black colleges and universities. Higher education leaders at all types of institutions will find the discussion of best practices for internationalization and international initiatives at HBCUs to be both useful and inspiring."

—Freeman A. Hrabowski, President, *University of Maryland, Baltimore County (USA)*

Made in the USA
Columbia, SC
16 April 2023